NOT TO FORGET

The Story of Harry Reiss and the Creation of
The Rockland Center for Holocaust Studies

By Marion Reiss

Library of Congress Reiss, Marion
"Not To Forget"   ISBN 2013 0-928-220-04-4

Printed and Published in the USA by The MP Press Inc.

DEDICATION

Dedicated to the Memory of the Six Million

And to the Memory of my Husband, Harry Reiss who devoted
much of his life, "Not to Forget"

TABLE OF CONTENTS

FOREWORD BY RABBI IRVING YITZ GREENBERG

Holocaust Scholar and Founding President of CLAL - National Jewish Center
for Learning and Leadership

Founder, Chairman, Professor of Jewish Studies at City University of New
York

This book is both an important contribution to history and a mitzvah. The historical significance lies in the fact that it is an account of the emergence of a new institution in Jewish life – the Holocaust Memorial Center. In Biblical times, the Temple, the priestly class, prophecy and kingship emerged as the major institutions of political and religious life. In the rabbinic period, prayer and the synagogue and the study hall [= yeshiva] with Rabbis as their spiritual leaders emerged to serve as the key channels of communal and religious life. In our time, this new institution is being created to communicate the nature and implications of this central event of Jewish history – the Shoah. The Center tells the story, draws lessons, educates the public, passes on the message to all. There are already dozens of such centers around the world. Someday, I believe that there will be one in every significant Jewish community. Future historians will search the records and sources to learn: how were such centers created? Who motivated them? What were they thinking? How did they get the public to back them?

This book, which tells the story of the Rockland County Center, will be a treasure trove for those future chroniclers of Jewish life. Here we have in meticulous and loving detail a description of a grass roots effort which successfully created a Center for Rockland

County. It gives us the roles of the various elements, the survivors and the non-survivors, the public authorities (many of them non-Jewish), the people and community groups that took responsibility. How we would give our right arm for a detailed account of the creation of the Talmudic academies such as Sura and Pumbedita. How much deeper would be our understanding of the impact of and role in personal life of sacrifices in Biblical times, if we had a parallel account to this book of how Shiloh or Beth El became regional religious centers before the great Temple in Jerusalem came into being.

This book then will not only be a source to turn to for learning what happened in Rockland. It will be combed over by historians trying to understand in depth how Jewish life grew and expressed itself in absorbing the fearsome, challenging event of the Holocaust so that it became part of a deepening Jewish culture in America.

This book is also a mitzvah. The Rashba (Rabbi Shlomo ben Aderet), one of the greatest halachists of medieval Jewry wrote that it is a mitzvah to publicize the doer of a mitzvah (based on the Torah's announcement that Reuven sought to save Joseph from being killed by his brothers (see Genesis 37:22). This book tells the story of Harry Reiss, the indispensable man in the creation of the Rockland Center for Holocaust Studies. Harry Reiss was not a survivor. He was American born. But at a time when there was not much attention to the Holocaust, he grasped how monumental it was, how powerful its impact and how essential it was to teach about the event and draw forth religious and moral lessons. Undoubtedly his religious feelings as an Orthodox Jew and his understanding of history and its role (he was a teacher of history in the New York School System) led him to this deep understanding. Harry instituted and taught a course on the Holocaust at Rockland Community College. Using his friendships and connections, he got the County to proclaim Holocaust

Remembrance Day – even before the national program was developed by President Carter's Presidential Commission on the Holocaust. He energized survivors who had been hesitant to expose their children or afraid to talk about their experiences in public to join the cause. He worked indefatigably to create community programs, and then an actual Center. For thirty years, he drew government officials, heads of civil organizations, Rabbis and educators, public school and private school teachers into an alliance that led to the successful creation of the Center. He spared no energy to help with the private fundraising – and obtaining public funding as well – so the Center could exist. The record of his efforts will be invaluable to historians of all the Holocaust Memorial work done in this country – for it gives a picture of how this process worked at the local community level. This account, written by his wife, Marion, as a labor of love, fulfills the mitzvah of publicizing a mitzvah of thirty years duration (and still going on after his death). The book illuminates the tireless effort, wisdom, relationship managing, community organizing and program development work of one man – even as it credits the contributions of the many who joined in and made the Center happen.

Thanks to Centers like the one depicted in this book, the sacred task of remembering the Shoah and the victims and the world that was destroyed is continuing. The moral challenge of working so that this catastrophe will never be allowed to happen again is being advanced all the time. As an Orthodox Jew who lived a total Jewish life, Harry Reiss never let his focus on the need to remember the Holocaust divert him from the larger picture of Judaism as a religion of hope and of life. The Center is therefore focused in its work on human rights and on the need for Americans to care for all whose life and freedom is threatened. Thus the Center shows how Jewish particular concerns, expressed with integrity and vision, bring protection for all humans and uphold life everywhere.

This book deserves to be read by everyone who treasures historical memory and ethical responsibility as well as those who understand that the Holocaust has become the benchmark for judging the moral dimensions of political, cultural and educational life in this era.

Rabbi Irving Yitz Greenberg

ENDORSEMENT BY DAVID S. WYMAN

Professor of History, Emeritus University of Massachusetts, Amherst

Author of "The Abandonment of the Jews:

America and the Holocaust, 1941-1945"

Until the 1960's, the American public in general had very limited knowledge of the Holocaust. Several developments in the 1960's and 1970's began to widen that knowledge. These included the trial of Adolf Eichmann in 1961, the publication of Night and other books by Elie Wiesel, and the efforts of many Holocaust survivors who had come to the United States after World War II. In 1978 an important turn point occurred with the four-night, prime-time TV miniseries Holocaust and the extremely heavy press coverage it received.

In the years that followed, the Holocaust became widely known throughout the United States. Annual "Days of Remembrance" spread across the nation. College and high school courses concerning the Holocaust became common. Many Holocaust museums and study centers, large and small, were established.

Marion Reiss has given us a valuable memoir and history of one of the earliest of the Holocaust Centers. Her sources are a historian's treasure trove – Basic primary materials: letters, notes, documents from across 30 years. She has provided a valuable piece

X

of a much larger picture, that of Americans concerned with understanding and learning from their nation's response to the Holocaust.

David S. Wyman
Professor of History, Emeritus
University of Massachusetts,
Amherst

May 3, 2013

Endorsement by Dr. David Marwell

Director of Museum of Jewish Heritage

A Living Memorial to the Holocaust

Not to Forget: The Story of Harry Reiss and the Creation of The Rockland Center for Holocaust Studies should be read by anyone interested in Holocaust commemoration in the United States. Predating the efforts that resulted in the United States Holocaust Memorial Museum in Washington and the Museum of Jewish Heritage – A Living Memorial to the Holocaust in New York City, the Rockland Center offers an example of individual initiative and dedication. More than simply a fascinating local history, this book provides insight into the entire question of Holocaust memory and the quest to preserve it.

ENDORSEMENT BY DR. CLIFF WOOD

President Rockland Community College

The Holocaust Museum and Study Center, formerly the Rockland Center for Holocaust Studies, exists because of the vision of Harry Reiss, who called a community to action to make certain that Holocaust history is not forgotten. He wanted the lessons of the Holocaust to be explored by and taught to the diverse community of Rockland County. Harry, who was a dedicated professor of Social Sciences at Rockland Community College for a number of years, inspired his students and colleagues as well as the larger community always to remember, not only the horrors of the Holocaust, but also the spirit, humanity and determination of those who were victimized, of those who endured, of those who survived, and of those heroes who hid and protected them and stood up to evil.

How fitting it is, then, that the Holocaust Museum and Study Center now finds a home at Rockland Community College, which Harry Reiss loved and where he devoted such passion and energy to educating others about the Holocaust. We at RCC are privileged to host the Holocaust Museum and Study Center on our campus and to play a role in continuing the important work and enduring legacy of Harry Reiss.

Endorsement by Rabbi Dr. Moshe Dovid Tendler

Rav, Community Synagogue of Monsey

Rosh Yeshiva, Rabbi Isaac and Bella Tendler Chair of Jewish Medical Ethics, Yeshiva University

The story of the phenomenal growth of the Jewish community in Monsey, New York will surely be written. At that time the major contributions of Mr. Harry Reiss (obm) to the Holocaust Museum and to uniting the community through the Holocaust Remembrance programs he chaired, will be properly acknowledged.

Moshe Dovid Tendler

Acknowledgments

After five years of bringing this work to fruition, I want to thank my editor and friend, Asher Goldstein, who worked through every phrase and word of the manuscript, and also gave freely of his advice.

I also want to thank Rabbi Dr. Moses D. Tendler for giving of his time to read through the manuscript and render his personal and halachic guidance.

I would like to give a special acknowledgment and tribute to my publisher, Manny Polak, whose invaluable expertise and advice in actually preparing this volume for publication made my dream into a reality. A special thank you to his wife, Helena, for her extraordinary patience and encouragement throughout the entire publication process.

Many others encouraged and helped me along the way. Sam Colman was always available to discuss a passage or an event on the phone and Jeff Weinberger gave me a smile and a "heads up" whenever over the five years I would tell him that I was still writing.

I want in particular to express my appreciation to my dear children, whose constant support and advice sustained me throughout a long and difficult process.

My son Rabbi Yona Reiss, who read through the manuscript several times and gave freely of his sagacious wisdom on matters large and small.

My daughter Linda Reiss-Wolicki, who gave judicious and sensible counsel on crucial issues.

My daughter Wendy Reiss Shindler, whose caring, moral support throughout was always a source of comfort and hope for me.

A special thanks to my grandson Michael Shindler for his artistic design for the cover.

Many thanks also to all those who read parts of the manuscript and offered their comments, including my cousin Rabbi Chaim Spring.

A special word of thanks also to Shaindy Zeide, whose meticulous work in the final typesetting and graphic placement was essential in preparing this work for publication.

Finally, I am most grateful to the Almighty, may His name be praised, for giving me the strength to confront this task and meet the challenge.

PREFACE

Memory fades and so much of the history of good people and world-altering events is lost in the passage of time.

The inspiration for the establishment of the Rockland Center can be traced to the determination of a man of singular purpose and dedication, a teacher, my dear husband OBM, Harry Reiss, who in his quiet and unassuming way galvanized a whole community to create and institutionalize a memorial to the victims of the Holocaust. It was his sincere belief that through teaching of the evils that were perpetuated in that horrific period, "man's inhumanity to man" might somehow be prevented in the future.

Harry was joined by equally dedicated individuals, particularly his two co-leaders in the evolution and progression of the Center, Dr. Harold Siegelbaum and Georgine Hyde. His idea was brought to fruition, too, through the efforts of a good friend, then-Chairman of the Rockland County Legislature and later New York Assemblyman and Ramapo Judge, Sam Colman.

Many others joined in this mission, and their names and stories are told in this book.

My impetus in writing this book was both intellectual and emotional. First of all, as someone who had been witness to the creation and development of the Center from the beginning, I would often be asked to recall significant names, dates, and events that had occurred in relation to the Center. Emotionally, the impetus became an injunction, albeit self-imposed, after my husband's suffering a severe stroke in 2006 and his passing away 18 months later.

A year after Harry's death in 2007, I attended a Kristallnacht Vigil at the New City Courthouse. It was a blistery cold day, almost like the one two years earlier which Harry had conducted and following which he had contracted a particularly severe form of pneumonia that lasted for several weeks. But now I could feel nothing. Despite the inclement weather, I remember not wearing a coat. After listening to speech after speech and remembering the role that Harry had played in these ceremonies, I walked off, away from the crowd, wanting to be alone with my thoughts. Somehow a photographer focused his camera on my facial expression, and my photograph appeared in the local paper the next day. When I complained to a friend, she asked, "Do you want to be invisible?" It was probably at that time that I decided that the history of the Holocaust Museum and Study Center, the name it now bore, should not be invisible, and so this written history began.

In deciding the format for this book, I had to choose between writing a memoir of Harry Reiss, my husband, or a straight history of the Center. Should it be in the first person or third? The answers came when I decided to do a trial chapter. I would just start to write and see what would emerge. I did just that, and the story flowed. What resulted was a remembrance of the creation of the Rockland Center for Holocaust Studies and of the players who walked across that particular stage of history. Since I became at times one of the players, I saw myself in third person, and that is how the format remained.

Along the way, I wondered at which point I should end this volume. There, too, the answer came one day when, after typing a sentence about the testimonial dinner in 2007, I sat back and realized that I had written the last sentence. And so the book ends right there. More recent events, though occasionally alluded to in the text, are recorded in the Epilogue.

INTRODUCTION

Many books have been written about the Holocaust, some being factual histories, but many more being personal memoirs and recollections.

In one of the first meetings of scholars of the Holocaust in the 1970's, held in a very hot, crowded and perhaps even smoke-filled room in Manhattan, in an atmosphere suffused with the electricity of birth of something new, Alexander Donat, who had written the seminal work on Treblinka, cautioned those of us in his audience about the infidelity of memory. From a purely historiographical perspective, the further removed one is from the event, the less reliable is the memory of it. Time may blur certain facts, mixing one event with another, even one face with a second, until we can no longer guarantee personal recollection as fact. Did a particular event occur as it was remembered? Or was it blurred with the personal recollection of another who had related it to the first person? How much more this ambiguity applies to recollections written not five or ten years after the event, but sixty!

And yet there seems to be a proliferation of remembrances of that devastating, traumatic period being published every year. Is this perhaps an expression of the final rendering of remembrance by those who fear that personal experiences may soon be lost as the survivors pass on, or is it more of a collection of remembered events mixed with stories retold by others, or, most worrisome, is it a reflection of a political agenda?

It was with some trepidation, therefore, that I undertook to recount the history of the establishment of one of the first Holocaust Centers in the New York Region, The Rockland Holocaust Museum and Study Center, housed in Rockland County. This volume weaves the history of the establishment of the Rockland Center for Holocaust Studies, as it was called for many years, from its inception as the Rockland Commission on the Holocaust in 1979 to its present title and incarnation. The history, the story, is told in the format of a memoir, recounting the seminal role played by my late husband, Harry Reiss, in the inception, development, and evolution of this institution. Much of the source material derives from his notes as the events were taking place.

I am empowered in this undertaking in part by another point of view, expressed by the noted Holocaust historian, Yehuda Bauer, in *Dimensions* magazine in 2004: "The fact that we view events from a subjective angle does not mean that these events did not happen, and there are ways of mitigating the influence of subjective factors so that the never-ending effort to get as close to the actual event as possible can yield satisfactory results (so) that we may come very close to a full understanding [of the subject]." In fact, Professor Bauer states elsewhere that "history can miss the centrally important evidence of the decision-making processes both for main institutions and ordinary individuals."

In documenting the history of the Rockland Center for Holocaust Studies, the formative name that is ingrained in me, I have used the vast collection of personal notes, photos, speeches, letters, documents, and newspaper articles that were in my husband's possession. As a memoir, I also incorporated my personal recollections of conversations, interactions, emotions, and drama that are part of my own personal memory. Nonetheless, at least from Bauer's comments, these elements have validity on revealing the processes of deliberation and decision that are essential to telling the story. It is my hope that both aspects will help the reader to extrapolate the essence of the development of Holocaust commemoration in the United States.

The history of Holocaust study is inextricably intertwined with the history of its institutionalization, most specifically with the creation of museums, study centers, and memorials designed to commemorate and memorialize.

Several things have occurred to me. First, that the original plans of those who design such memorials often undergo much change by the time the memorial is completed. Second, that the trials and tribulations in the birth and development of such commemorating organizations seem to be far more exaggerated in intensity and drama than those experienced by non-Holocaust institutions. Finally there seems to be an underlying tension that both binds and tears apart those working together to create and perpetuate such memorials. I have thought this was perhaps due to the horrendous nature of the subject itself, which overpowers and puts into the shadow those who work in its cause; or perhaps it is due to the survivors themselves when they are part of the establishing group as often they are, their memories fresh or unspoken constituting an underbelly of pain, rising and subsiding like the swells in the sea, that affect all involved in the undertaking.

A pattern in the formation of Holocaust institutions nonetheless emerges, beginning with inspiration, usually spearheaded by a few survivors who want to create a memorial to those who died in the Holocaust, followed or accompanied by the desire for commemoration, and ending in the establishment of a study center or museum. These stages may occur sequentially or, as was the case with the Rockland Center for Holocaust Studies, concurrently. The museum stage may grow to include other historically or currently related exhibits of Jewish and/or humanitarian interest.

Another example of this memorialization is the museum of Jewish Heritage – A Living Memorial to the Holocaust (these existing names having been reversed immediately before its opening in 1997), housed in Battery Park at the foot of Manhattan. Initially, there was to be a monument built in Riverside Park, and indeed a plaque is still embedded there at 83rd Street. Then there arose the idea of a commemoration in the form of an annual Yom HaShoah event. Finally, the plan for building the Museum at Battery Park became so overriding a goal that groundbreaking for the expansion of the structure took place soon after the events of September 11, 2001.

With several of these questions in mind, and with a huge body of untouched primary source material at my disposal, I decided to attempt to record in the interests of historical investigation the rise and development of Rockland County's Holocaust memorial. My sources, as mentioned, are mainly the personal notes of my late husband, Harry Reiss, who was one of the founders of the center and its initial proponent, correspondence associated with the creation of the center and museum, newspaper clippings and articles recording its development, and the boxes of minutiae meticulously kept by Harry in his years as executive director and secretary of the institution.

I hope that this volume may serve as a primary source of information for those who might undertake a more scholarly study of the formation of Holocaust museums in the United States and that it will add to the body of knowledge already recorded in such volumes as "Preserving Memory – The Struggle to Create America's Holocaust Museum" and "Never Too Late to Remember – The Politics Behind New York City's Holocaust Museums." It will be interesting to see whether the "struggles," indeed the "politics," involved in building Holocaust memorials differ from the building of other museums. If this is found to be the case, we will want to know the nature of the difference and whether this difference may be attributed to the subject matter.

I therefore submit the following history of the Holocaust Museum and Study Center, perhaps better known to some as the Rockland Center for Holocaust Studies, as a personal memoir of the wife of Harry Reiss, who inspired its birth and bore its ideals for some thirty years. To paraphrase an historical truism: "History is what happened to other people; memory is what happened to ourselves." I hope this volume will fulfill both elements, history and memory.

CHAPTER 1

THE BEGINNING
The Establishment of the Holocaust Commission
Choosing a Site
The First Holocaust Remembrance Day Program

"In Tadeuzc Borowki's book, *This Way for the Gas, Ladies and Gentleman*, a young non-Jew stationed as a helper at the Auschwitz concentration camp writes about the almost pastoral setting of his surroundings. Kicking a soccer ball around to pass the time, with flowers blooming beside the barracks, he watches a train of boxcars arrive with Jews, some of the women wearing summer dresses believing they were being transported for 'resettlement.' With his attention momentarily diverted by the soccer ball, the youth turns around and finds everyone gone, and realizes that 3,000 people have passed to their deaths."

So began the presentation of the Holocaust Remembrance Day program in Rockland County on April 13, 1980, by Harry Reiss, continuing for the next 18 years. And so, perhaps, we find the explanation of how this American-born history teacher, perhaps thinking of his own childhood growing up in New York and playing ball under the same beautiful blue sky while millions of Jews were being murdered in Europe, came to feel that it was his personal obligation to teach and memorialize the lessons of the Holocaust.

On April 13, 1978, *The Journal News*, a Rockland County, NY, daily, published its first article on Rockland's commemoration of the Holocaust in an article entitled, "Teaching the Lessons of the Past."

"He wasn't even there [In Europe]," the article noted, "but what happened there causes great emotions, silences, and a struggle to hide the tears. Harry Reiss of Monsey is a history teacher in the New York City School system. An orthodox Jew in his late 40's, he has been teaching a course for two years at Rockland Community College on the Holocaust – The Persecution and Destruction of Six Million European Jews by the German Nazis under Adolf Hitler's régime from 1933 to 1945.

Courtesy of The Journal News

"'Most people have an appalling ignorance of history,' said Reiss, 'for many young people, studying the Holocaust is like studying ancient history. Even in the orthodox community where many are Holocaust survivors or children of survivors, there are factual inaccuracies of what really happened.' To rectify the situation, Reiss wrote to Dr. Sue Commandy, assistant coordinator of the Israel and Judaic Studies programs at Rockland Community College, suggesting the possibility of teaching a course on the Holocaust. He said he had mixed emotions about the television series, 'Shoah,' and resented any recounting of the attempted annihilation of an entire people presented as a slick media event. 'You can't sum up in three words the destruction of one-third of a people that has existed for 5,000 years,' he explained. 'For orthodox Jews, the Holocaust is a minor thing even though it happened to them. Their religion is one of hope, and their view of the world is progressive. They commemorate the Holocaust but they reason that if only 10 Jews were left in the world, it would still be enough and that God's work would still be carried on. They don't dwell on the past. So for many, the facts about the Holocaust are forever lost. You can react to the Holocaust in one of three ways: you can deny it ever happened, you can say forget about it, or you can bear witness because it did happen and you must see that it doesn't happen again.'"

It was shortly after this article appeared that Reiss, on one of the last days of the Passover holiday, took a long walk in Viola Park, nearby his home in the County, with his friend and neighbor Sam Colman,- then Chairman of Rockland County Legislature and later a New York State Assemblyman. Out of their conversation grew the idea of the County Legislature's issuing a proclamation declaring April 28-29, the anniversary of the liberation of Dachau, one of the infamous death camps, as Holocaust Remembrance Days in Rockland County.

Almost a year to the day after the appearance of the *Journal News* article, Kevin Coupe, a staff writer for that paper, reported on April 27, 1979, on the Rockland County Legislatures proclamation, co-signed by its chairman, Colman, a Democrat, and John Murphy, a Republican. The proclamation scroll was accepted jointly by Reiss and Georgine Hyde, then a member and late a chairperson of the East Ramapo, New York School district and herself a Holocaust survivor. Other Holocaust survivors also witnessed the event at the County

3

Courtesy of The Journal News

Holocaust survivors meet with Legislator John Murphy, second from left, and Legislature Chairman Sam Colman, who examines proclamation with Georgine Hyde and Harold Reiss.

Government office. As Reiss had said a year earlier, remembering was sometimes difficult even for those who had lived through the Holocaust. Sala Kirschner, a survivor, affirmed that "remembrance of the past is difficult if you are a survivor of a Nazi concentration camp. Because we don't want to live in the past, we have not given it to our children. We don't want to live it again. It's the only way to survive." But Georgine Hyde added poignantly, "The survivors hope they can make enough of an impression to ensure a Holocaust never occurs again. This [proclamation] is a small debt to pay to those we left behind. Those who did not return would want us to take this opportunity to explain this portion of history."

Later that year, when a meeting convened by Reiss was held at a Ramapo High School to obtain support for the building of the Holocaust Study Center, Hyde would stand up and declare that she had never told her own son, who was then 17 years old, of her experiences in the Holocaust. Echoing Sala Kirschner, Georgine Hyde said her aim had been to look to the future, not the past. Now, however, she realized that her son should have been told everything so as not to allow these things to happen again.

4

Sam Colman's wife had lived the first five years of her life in a concentration camp and her father had been killed before she ever knew him Sam now announced plans to set up a Holocaust Commission that would be charged with "devising some permanent remembrance of the Holocaust based on the Commission set up on a national level by president Jimmy Carter." The members of that commission were Harry Reiss, Administrative Director; with Georgine Hyde and Dr. Harold Siegelbaum of Nyack as co-chairpersons. Little did those three Rockland residents have any idea of the paths they would take and the accomplishments that would accrue from their efforts. In summing up the establishment of the Commission, Sam Colman stated: "The whole purpose is to educate the public as to what happened." John Murphy agreed and added, "I don't believe what took place was a tragedy for the Jews only. I believe it was a tragedy for all human beings."

Even before the Rockland Proclamation was issued, Harry Reiss had written to Congressman Stephen Solarz of New York, who had been appointed to President Carter's Commission on the Holocaust, for information about the United States Proclamation of Remembrance. Congressman Solarz replied early in April, sending a copy of the U.S. Proclamation, which Harry gave to Sam Colman.

A week later, Rockland County Resolution #281, modeled on the Federal Resolution, was proposed by Colman and Murphy and unanimously accepted by the County Legislature on May 15, 1979. The resolution established "A Commission on the Holocaust," formally appointed "Mrs. Georgine Hyde of Pomona and Dr. Harold Siegelbaum of West Nyack to be co-chairpersons of this Commission and Mr. Harry Reiss, RCC Adjunct Professor on the Holocaust as member and Administrative Director to the Commission." It called for recommendations to be made within 60 days to the Rockland County legislature as to the size and full composition of the

5

Commission, as well as recommendations "on how to Commemorate and how to Memorialize this tragic period in Human History." The Commission was to complete its work no later than June 1980. Reiss was to hold the unpaid administrative position for the next ten years.

The Rockland County Commission on the Holocaust (in formation) held its first meeting on May 17, 1979, with an agenda outlining the establishment, function, advisory groups, and suggestions for memorial. (The agenda, as Reiss noted, was based on the U.S. Holocaust Commission resolution.) Brian Miele, Mayor of the village of Hillburn, was one of the first to join the newly established Commission "so that horrendous act of inhumanity will never be forgotten." The next meeting was held at the County Office Building in New City on June 14. That meeting proposed the initial membership of the commission, and on July 9, Reiss reported to Sam Colman in what the Administrative Director termed the "first letter" on the formal recommendation that the Commission consist of 15 members: in addition to Hyde, Siegelbaum, and Reiss, the members would include Reverend Robert Battles Jr., Pastor of the Germonds Presbyterian Church; Monsignor James Cox, Vicar of Rockland County; Honorable Kenneth Gribetz, District Attorney of Rockland County; Dr. Seymour Eskow, President of Rockland Community College; Mr. Irving Kintisch, member of the Jewish War Veterans and among the Dachau concentration camp liberators; honorable Brian Miele, Mayor of the Village of Hillburn; Rabbi Paul Schuchalter, Rabbi of Congregation Sons of Israel, Suffern, and representative of the Rockland County Board of Rabbis; Judge Morton Silberman, State Supreme Court; and Rabbi Dr. Moses Tendler, Rabbi of Community Synagogue of Monsey.

The full Commission plenum held its first meeting in the Law Library of the County Office Building on November 7, 1979. Prior to that assembly, a recommendation was drafted to add two Advisory

6

Committees to the Commission, one on Education and one representing a Survivors group. A press release went out announcing these additions the day after the meeting.

By November 1979, the Commission was planning a variety of commemorations. *The Journal News* reported in an article on November 22, written by Kevin Coupe on November 22:

"The Rockland County Commission on the Holocaust is widening its plans and expectations. Commission Administrative Director [Harry] Reiss said this week that a variety of commemorations are currently in the planning stages. 'We expect to have our plans pretty well set by June when we have to report to the County Legislature.' Reiss said. Among the proposals being studied for cost and practicality by the commission are: the establishment of a living memorial or a museum–library resource center featuring memorabilia from the Holocaust donated by county survivors; the compilation of a tape library which would feature oral reflections on the Holocaust by the people who survived it; the preparation of a 10th-grade curriculum guide which could be used by local school districts and private institutions in teaching the Holocaust, and finally the creation of

Harold Siegelbaum, Sam Colman, Harry Reiss, Georgine Hyde, Leo Kelmar, and Ilse Loeb

some sort of permanent memorial to the Holocaust which would be situated at some point in the county. It was this latter charge that was foremost in the mandate that the Legislature had given the Commission by the Legislature last Spring. 'Right now, the memorial is perhaps the most vague plan,' Reiss said. 'It could be a plaque or a [statue] or an abstract work of art. We'll have to commission that, but we will be doing it all through private donations. We haven't asked the county for any money, and we don't intend to.'

"The living memorial referred to by Reiss is planned for either a public library in the county or at Rockland Community College, he said, with a variety of preliminary discussions currently in progress. 'Much of the planning for it is being handled by a committee of Holocaust survivors,' Reiss said. 'As many as forty county residents who survived the Nazis have begun contributing their time to the Commission. We estimate that there are probably thousands of survivors living in the county right now.'

"Reiss said that the curriculum guide is being targeted at 10th-grade students because that seems to be when world and European history are studied most frequently. The commission hopes that in addition to preparing tapes and a guide to the Holocaust tragedy, a speakers bureau of local residents can be established. 'We'd like to send out speakers and programs to any schools and churches that want one,' he said. 'We have an Education Committee that is quite far along, with representatives from almost every school district in the county, plus private schools that are both gentile and Jewish.'

"Originally, a fund-raising goal of between $10,000 and $15,000 was anticipated," Reiss said. 'At the moment we don't know how much we're going to need, but it'll be more than the

$15,000. We'll probably be going after grant money from private institutions, but we'd rather have small donations from a lot of people than a few big donations.' Reiss said that he can envision a day sometime in the future when a county memorial to the Holocaust will be dedicated. 'There would be thousands of local survivors there,' he said, 'many committed to keeping the memory of Holocaust alive in the hope that it would never happen again. There would be people there who were in concentration camps with Anne Frank, people who went to school with her in the Netherlands, people who survived the sadistic horror of Dr. Josef Mengele. That would be quite a day,' he said."

There was a survivor in Rockland County by the name of Marc Berkowitz, who lived in an apartment near Valley Cottage and who presented a packet of his memoirs to the Commission. He had been one of Mengele's twins. The effort of speaking about the past seemed too much for him to bear, and he stopped coming to meetings of the survivors group. At that time, the chair of the survivors group, Leo Kelmar, would bring Marc to the group's meetings. Mr. Berkowitz and his wife later attended the World Gathering of Holocaust Survivors in 1981, along with Harry Reiss.

Harry thought it would be a good idea to locate the proposed Study Center in a public place. At that time, there was a little-used annex to the Finkelstein Memorial Library, which housed a few offices on its upper floor and a little storage area. Reiss began talking with the Director of the Library, Sam Simon, about the possibility of using this space. Sam was very enthusiastic at the idea and made plans to bring the matter before the library's board of directors. Meantime, other venues were suggested. Dr. Mendy Ganchrow, a prominent Monsey physician, suggested that since the Holocaust was a Jewish tragedy, the center should be located in a Jewish place. His particular choice was the Hebrew Institute of Rockland County

(HIROC), now called ASHAR (Adolph Schreiber Hebrew Academy of Rockland), located on Highview Road, off College Road. Harry disagreed, arguing that the Study Center should be intended for all students, regardless of religion, and that many people would hesitate going to a Jewish Day School or any other religious setting. Another person who questioned the Finkelstein Library location proposal at first was Rabbi Morton Summer, who had been a former principal of HIROC and was then on the library's board of trustees. Rabbi Summer expressed the understandable sentiment of many people in those days that the Holocaust was a profoundly Jewish experience and should not be diluted by placing anything related to it in a secular setting. Still another person voicing concerns about the location was Alice Golar, also a member of the library's board; however, her reasons were diametrically opposite those of Rabbi Summer's. She was not sure that anything so particularly Jewish should be housed in the Finkelstein Library, which was a public facility. Nevertheless, Rabbi Summer later became one of the Center's most passionate supporters; and Alice Golar enthusiastically participated in the groundbreaking ceremony several years later, when the library annex became the permanent home of the Rockland Center for Holocaust Studies. In fact, the actual library board resolution passed in October 29, 1981 to "confirm its support of a Rockland Center for Holocaust Studies to be established at the Finkelstein Memorial Library" was moved by "Mr. Summer and seconded by Mrs. Golar."

Rockland Community College was also suggested as a location possibility, as there was indeed a model for this idea; the Center for Holocaust Studies, directed by Dr. Yaffa Eliach, at Brooklyn College. Harry was not opposed to that idea, but space was a problem at the Rockland College. Gradually momentum gathered for the Finkelstein Library annex: it was available and the proposal had the support of the library's director.

One public meeting, held on September 22, 1981, especially stood out in the discussions about a site. The library's annex, as it happened, was the venue of the debate, and it was packed with supporters and detractors of the proposed location of the Holocaust Studies Center. At one point, a gentleman quietly raised his hand and asked to speak. It was County Treasurer Joe St. Lawrence, who in a few well-chosen words turned the discussion around. In essence he said: "How can anyone who has witnessed the horrors of the Nazi genocide not support the dissemination of information about the history that took place?" His eloquence and support, unsolicited and genuinely motivated by his own moral outrage at the horrific events composing the Holocaust, provided the persuasive factor in the Commissions favoring the library annex as the location for the Rockland Center for Holocaust Studies. The renovated building became its permanent home.

Concurrently with the negotiations over a home for the Center, plans were being formulated for the first county-wide commemoration ceremony, to be held on April 13, 1980. There being as yet no official center or location for the Holocaust Center and its

Courtesy of The Journal News

Georgine Hyde, Judge William Zeck and Harry Reiss examine commemorative program

11

Commission, all meetings were held at the Reiss home. Marion and Harry hosted the members of the Remembrance Day Committee in their living room and dining room that year and then for the next 18 years. The Reiss's living room often turned into a studio, with a screen being set up to view slides and a tape recorder played to listen to audio-visual materials that were being considered for the forthcoming event. Mailings were prepared in the finished basement, a Ping-Pong table serving as the work bench for folding, collating, stuffing and stamping activities.

That first year, and for several years thereafter, there was no budget for any of this. Harry used to go around asking friends and neighbors for small donations to cover printing and mailing costs. He remembered the first time he approached one neighbor to request a donation. When asked "How much?" Harry tentatively answered, "$100." The neighbor laughed and said, "That's all?" and immediately wrote a check. Reiss also bargained with the printers and vendors for the lowest price possible if not for an outright donation of their services. It was a hand-to-mouth operation that went on for years.

The work of advertising the new Holocaust Center and the Remembrance Day events was never easy. The committee had to rely on its own footwork to get the word out. For instance, Harry and his family personally distributed flyers to all synagogues and organizations in the County, and many a Sunday was spent with Marion and the Reiss children putting up posters on store windows. Permission to display the posters and flyers had first to be obtained from proprietors, and some stores allowed the material to be propped up only in a corner. Committee members quickly learned, too, that they could not leave posters at just any location, no matter how sincere the promise was to "put it up later." They had to check to be sure the material was displayed, sometimes returning over and over again doing whatever was necessary to see to it that the advertising was on view in prominent places. Helpfully, some organizations would include the flyers in their own mailings if they received them quickly enough. It was always a race, it seemed, to get the packages of flyers to the right place.

If mailings were expensive and ways of their subvention had to be found, the same was true of speakers at Remembrance events. It was made clear that they were expected to contribute their time, and for the most part in those early years they did. At times, there were unavoidable out-of-pocket expenses, such as for custodial help in the high school where the programs were held. Apparently, though, not everyone connected with the Center was apprised of, or was concerned about, its financial problems. It came as a big shock sometime down the road, when sodas were once ordered for an event, and the person in charge had paid a high price for the cold drinks. Harry Reiss questioned the expense, since he had always negotiated for an outright donation or a reduced price. The answer he received was: "What do you care? The organization is paying for it not you." The Reisses and several other Commission members, told of this exchange, were shocked by such a reaction after all their years of saving money for the organization. For Marion Reiss, at least, this became a turning point in the transformation of the Center from an "inspiration" to an "organization".

The Remembrance Day Committee began work on a formula for its first event, which was to stay constant for the next 18 years. There would be a presentation of colors. The first year, the honor was offered to the Jewish War Veterans, but a problem arose: that organization wanted the right to speak at the commemoration about the JWV. This was a touchy point that eventually led to severing ties with these veterans, because Harry and the committee were adamant in not diluting the commemoration of the Holocaust and the memorial to its victims by giving any perk, political or otherwise, to any organization for its participation. This was a novel idea at the time, when credit was demanded and given at almost every public and organizational event in the county. But the Remembrance Day Committee was insistent; no dignitaries or public officials were to be mentioned: the dignity of the event was to be maintained at whatever cost. Again, this was something new for the many public officials who attended such events; however, they seemed to understand, for they continued to support and attend every single commemoration.

Similarly people would arrive the day of the event with a special plea for a good cause, but they were consistently denied. This may have created animosity among some, but the commemoration was primary and the committee would not swerve from its ideals. On one occasion, a well-known national reporter arrived and wanted to be recognized to promote a worthy cause in which she was involved. One of the committee members, Janice Kalish, gave the reporter's proposal short shrift and stood ground for the rest of the committee. The incident may not have won Janice as a friend, but the would-be speaker recalled it years later, and remembered the commemoration with respect.

The colors were followed by an invocation by a clergyman. In the beginning years, Harry was careful to invite clergymen of different faiths to give the opening invocation. The first year there were three invocations, by Monsignor James Cox, who was a great supporter of the Holocaust Center and a member of its first board; Reverend Weldon McWilliams of Spring Valley; and Rabbi Paul Schuchalter of Suffern. In later years, the invocation was rotated among different denominations of the Jewish faith.

At the early ceremonies, photographs of paintings by artist David Friedman were displayed. His daughter, Miriam Morris, lived with her husband and children on a hilltop in the Rockland village of

Work Detail — David Friedman

©1987 Miriam Friedman Morris

Pomona. Her father had survived the camps and painted what he had seen there. After his death, she sought to have his paintings recognized and asked Reiss and the newly emerging Center for help. Eventually, his paintings were displayed at Yad Vashem in Jerusalem and at the Holocaust Museum in Washington, DC. Some of them were also displayed in Philadelphia at the Churches Conference on the Holocaust (which the Reisses as representatives of the Rockland Holocaust Center attended every year that this event was held on the East Coast). Much later, after personal tragedy had stuck her family, Miriam Morris donated a vast part of the collection to a museum in Europe. But those were the early days, when all was new and anything was or seemed possible.

In addition to copies of Friedman's artworks, Harry obtained a set of 50 posters from Yad Vashem titled, "Holocaust and Resistance," on the history of the Holocaust. The members of the Remembrance Day Committee, Janice and Larry Kalish, worked hand in hand with the Reiss family to put these posters up in the hallway leading to the auditorium in Ramapo High School every year.

Janice Kalish and Marion Reiss

The first commemoration event, called the Rockland County Remembrance Program dedicated to the victims of the Holocaust," finally materialized and took place on Sunday afternoon, April 13, 1980, at 2 P.M. at Ramapo Senior High School on Viola Road in Spring Valley. The commemoration committee wanted to involve as many groups in the community as possible in the event. A youth choir seemed like a good idea, and the Ramapo High School choral group sang. In later years, the ASHAR children's choir performed. Several children from ASHAR read poetry regarding the Holocaust. Why not have a dramatic reading by an adult, too? It was suggested. Reiss thought of the actor Steven Hill, who lived in the community and was a member of a very orthodox community in Monsey. He had been starring in the hit TV series, "Mission Impossible," but was replaced as the lead mainly because of the requirements of his Sabbath-observing religious life style. He soon thereafter obtained the starring role of the District Attorney on the popular "Law and Order" TV series. Hill came to the Reiss home, spoke with Harry for several hours about the Holocaust and the planned commemoration and, getting up to leave, agreed to do a dramatic reading that he would select himself. This turned out to be one of the longer presentations of the event and, together with the choir, the children's readings, and the main speaker, greatly extended the program. The main speaker at that initial event was Judge William Zeck, who shared his experiences as a young lawyer at the Nuremberg Trials. In addition to the choir, there were musical renditions by two students and by Cantor David Rosenzweig from the Jewish Community Center in Spring Valley.

The emotional highlight of the afternoon was perhaps the candle-lighting ceremony, introduced by survivor and Center co-president, Georgine Hyde. All survivors in the audience were invited to come up to the stage and light a candle in memory of those who had perished in the Shoah, the Hebrew term for the Holocaust.

Members of the Remembrance committee stood at the foot of the stage and distributed the candles to those who participated. Almost half of the audience slowly and in silence came to the stage to light a candle. Cantor Rosenzweig chanted the "Kel Maleh Rachamim" (God of mercy) memorial prayer.

This format of the program continued for the 18 years that Harry Reiss chaired this event, with his introduction, the presentation of the colors, accompanied by the salute to the flag and the national anthem, a musical selection, a keynote speaker, either an audio-visual presentation or a reading, the candle-lighting ceremony, and farewell remarks. But it was the candle-lighting that remained in everyone's minds as the most moving moment of the commemoration. In subsequent years, *yahrzeit* (memorial) candles, encased in jars, were substituted for plain candles, wrapped in little aluminum foil for the sake of safety. Much later, Holocaust Day events substituted six survivors to represent the entire group and the six million who perished in the Shoah to light candles. Although this latter format became the more accepted mode in later years, the raw power of survivors and sometimes their children coming up to the stage in great numbers was clear and moving testimony to the tragic events that had transpired.

At the first commemoration event, Sam Colman and John Grant, who was at that time Chairman of the Rockland County Legislature presented a proclamation to Harry Reiss declaring "April 13 and 14, 1980 as Days of Remembrance of Victims of The Holocaust in the County of Rockland."

The Remembrance committee had not known what to expect in terms of attendance despite the distribution of flyers and announcements throughout Rockland County. As the 2 PM opening ceremony approached, they waited expectantly in the huge auditorium, still sparsely occupied. Then slowly, with inexorable steadiness, people began streaming in, coming in pairs and threesomes and small groups until the main part of the auditorium was filled. The custodians opened the two wings, which filled up as well. There were nearly 800 people that first Remembrance Sunday and this attendance figure was to be repeated for two decades to come. There was a hush in the audience as Harry Reiss took the podium and opened with the words "kicking a soccer ball..."

Richard Laudor of *The Journal News* captured the essence of the event on April 14, in his account of what took place:

"They came to Ramapo High School Sunday to remember. Hundreds of Rocklanders, many wearing skullcaps, many wearing crosses around their necks, crammed in the Monsey school

auditorium to the rear walls, their jaws set to bear the anguish of memory while their lips trembled with the pain or recollection. Rev. Msgr. James Cox, Roman Catholic vicar of Rockland, stated in his invocation, 'The Holocaust must always be to us a tragic event whose dimensions are not diminished by the passage of time.' Rabbi Paul Schuchalter of Congregation Sons of Israel, Suffern: 'We can only honor [our dead] by every person adopting one soul and working that much harder to replace the soul that we lost.' Rev. Sidney Curry of the first Baptist Church, Spring Valley, added a plea for understanding: 'We have to use this as a way to show us how to get our world together,' he said. But the grim purpose of the day was presented by County Court Judge William Zeck in his keynote address. Zeck, one of about 120 American lawyers involved in the prosecution of Nazi war criminals at Nuremberg 30 years ago, emphasized that the conditions that created the Holocaust penetrated every sector of pre-war Germany 'It was not only the mad political leaders,' Zeck said, 'The physicians collaborated, the lawyers and judges collaborated, the businessmen and the bankers, the teachers and the educators, all collaborated to work on those ovens. The four-power courts indicted dozens of Nazi leaders for crimes against peace, crimes of war, and crimes against humanity, the death and torture of the Holocaust... The overwhelming important thing we did in those trials was to create a permanent history of the origins, development, and growth of the Nazi state and the perfidies and atrocities it imposed...We failed to establish as a crime the committing of genocide in one's homeland...but we made the effort and the effort was the most we could have done.' One more thing could be done Sunday, though, and that was to remember. As Georgine Hyde, a Holocaust survivor lit a candle in memory of the victims, everyone remembered."

Weeks later the Remembrance committee met to review what had happened. They felt that history had been made in Rockland County and perhaps in the entire area. This had been the region's first public, county-wide commemoration of the events of the Holocaust to take place, and it set the stage for the work of the Holocaust Commission in setting up Rockland's Holocaust Study Center. Along with the euphoria of having done something unique and having set a precedent, there was the more practical realization that the program would have to be shortened in the future. The formula of one hour and fifteen minutes was set down at that time and maintained throughout Reiss's tenure.

There were those, however, who found reason to question first the broad base of the Holocaust Commission and even the need for remembrance at all. Reiss responded to the first objection in an op-ed piece in *The Journal News*, published on September 16, 1980, entitled, "An Eternal Focus on the Holocaust". He wrote:

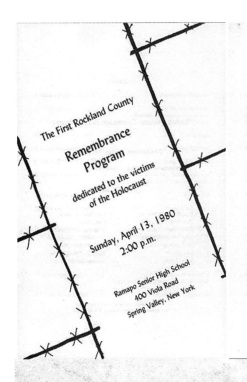

The First Rockland County

Remembrance
Program

dedicated to the victims
of the Holocaust

Sunday, April 13, 1980
2:00 p.m.

Ramapo Senior High School
400 Viola Road
Spring Valley, New York

ACKNOWLEDGEMENTS

We wish to express our deep gratitude to those private individuals and organizations whose generous contributions made this Remembrance Day Program possible.

Rockland County Commission
on the Holocaust

Remembrance Day Program Committee

Warren Berbit	Saul Kalish
Marc Berkowitz	Harry Reiss
Barbara Grau	Marion Reiss
Georgine Hyde	Manning Schwartz
Leo Kelmar	Dr. Harold Siegelbaum
Janice Kalish	

A SPECIAL NOTE OF THANKS TO THE SURVIVORS ADVISORY COMMITTEE FOR THEIR TIRELESS EFFORTS IN HELPING WITH SETTING UP THE PROGRAM.

Rockland County Commission on the Holocaust

Co-Chairmen:	Hon. Georgine Hyde
	Dr. Harold L. Siegelbaum
Administrative Director:	Harry Reiss

Commissioners

Rev. Robert Battles, Jr.	Hon. Brian L. Miele
Rev. Msg. James Cox	Harry Reiss
Dr. Seymour Eskow	Rabbi Paul Schuchalter
Hon. Kenneth Gribetz	Dr. Harold L. Siegelbaum
Hon. Georgine Hyde	Judge Morton Silberman
Leo Kelmar	Rabbi Dr. Moses Tendler
Irving Kintisch	Bernard Weiner

*The Commission was established by resolution of
the Legislature of Rockland County, May 15th, 1979.*

PROGRAM

1. *Salute to the Colors*	Jewish War Veterans
2. *Invocation*	Rabbi Paul Schuchalter
	Reverend Monsignor James Cox
	Reverend Weldon McWilliams
3. *Introductory Remarks*	Harry Reiss
4. *Presentation of Proclamation*	Hon. Sam Colman
5. *Address*	Judge William Zeck
6. *Choral Selection*	Ramapo Senior High School students
	under direction of Michael Fiorello
7. *Dramatic Reading*	Steven Hill
8. *Oboe and Piano Duet*	David Aron, Oboe
	Holly Shiffman, Piano
9. *Poems written by*	read by students of
children in the camps	Adolph Schreiber Hebrew Academy
	of Rockland
10. *Candle-lighting Ceremony*	Georgine Hyde
in memory of Holocaust Victims	
11. *Cantorial Liturgy*	Cantor David Rosenzweig
	Mitchel Rosenzweig, piano accompaniment
12. *Concluding Remarks*	Dr. Harold L. Siegelbaum

"A letter to the editor Sept. 8, questioned the non-sectarian and ecumenical nature of the Rockland County Commission on the Holocaust. The letter exhibited an appalling ignorance of the commission and of the historical significance of the Holocaust for the future of mankind.

"When the Rockland County Legislature unanimously created the commission on May 15, 1979, it patterned it after the President's Commission on the Holocaust, which was established by the President in November, 1978. The commission members, all of whom served without pay of any kind, were charged with recommending to the legislature and the people of the county how best to commemorate and how to memorialize this tragic period in human history. This obligation weighed heavily on the commission and informed all of its actions and recommendations.

"In the year of its existence to June 30, 1980, the commission sponsored a number of appropriate activities and events. On April 13, 1980, the commission sponsored the first Remembrance Day, dedicated to the victims of the Holocaust and held at Ramapo High School. In speech, music, poetry and dramatic reading and in a memorial candle-lighting ceremony, the thought stressed was that these horrible events should never be allowed to happen again... The memory of those killed in the Holocaust is indeed sacred not only to the commission members but to all Americans who are attempting to make sure that such events are never repeated. The question is sometimes asked 'Could such a catastrophe ever happen again in America?' It is precisely the ecumenical response to the commission that may provide the answer."

Earlier, in a letter to the editor on April 22, 1980, Harry had expressed his feelings about the first Remembrance event:

"It was a memorable and moving community experience to see the hundreds of Rockland County citizens of all faiths and ages who filled the auditorium of Ramapo High School in Spring Valley on Sunday, April 13, 1980, for the County's first Remembrance program dedicated to the victims of the Holocaust. The question is sometimes asked: 'Why is it necessary to be reminded of the Holocaust again?' One answer was given in the Journal News of April 19, in which a short news item listed a proposed 'Hitlerfest' in North Carolina to commemorate the anniversary of Hitler's birth! Potential and actual inhumanity of man to man is far from dead. To forget the errors of the past is to allow those errors to persist into the future. Daniel Webster stated 'G-d grants liberty to those who love it and are always ready to guard and defend it.' The outpouring of community interest and support for what we hope will become an annual Remembrance Day program and for the future goals of the county Commission on the Holocaust, including the establishment of a living memorial center for Holocaust studies in the county, show that American decency and belief in democracy are both alive and well in Rockland County."

Alan Weissberg, director of Secondary Education for the East Ramapo School District, wrote to Harry: "Organizing an event for the first time is always a difficult task. You were however able to put together an excellent Holocaust Remembrance program, which was very well attended. Our entire community has benefited from your hard work and capable administration. Harry, it was a pleasure dealing with you. We in East Ramapo were pleased to be closely associated with the Holocaust Remembrance program. You and the other wonderful people on the Holocaust Commission have undertaken a vital cause. We must never let the world forget what has occurred."

Sam Simon, director of the Finkelstein Memorial Library, also sent a letter of congratulations to Harry "on the successful Holocaust Commission Program" and indicated the next step: "The Library's architect, Walter Leicht, will be discussing the project with the Board. I would suggest a meeting soon between Mr. Gerstenfeld, Mr. Joseph's architect and Mr. Leicht." So began a new stage of the Holocaust Commission, or Council – that of establishing a Center.

Referral No. 5627
5/15/79

RESOLUTION NO.   281   OF 1979
ESTABLISHING A ROCKLAND COUNTY COMMISSION
ON THE HOLOCAUST

Colman/Murphy/unanimous

WHEREAS, President Carter has appointed a Presidential Commission of distinguished Americans to make recommendations to him and to the Congress on ways and means to Memorialize the period in Human History known as the Holocaust, when 6 million Jews and millions of other people had been exterminated by the Nazis in Europe, and

WHEREAS, the people of the United States should recognize that all acts of bigotry are rooted in the cruelty of spirit and the callousness that led the Nazis to commit atrocities against millions of people, and should dedicate themselves to the principle of human equality, and

WHEREAS, the people of the United States should recognize that tyranny creates the political atmosphere in which bigotry flourishes, and should be vigilant to detect, and ready to resist, the tyrannical exercise of power, and

WHEREAS, it is desirable that Rockland County establish a Commission known as the Commission on the Holocaust to work in parallel with the National Commission and to make recommendations of how Rockland County can commemorate this tragic period in Human History, and

WHEREAS, the Budget and Finance Committee of this Legislature has met, considered and approved this resolution, now, therefore, be it

RESOLVED, that the Legislature of Rockland County hereby establishes a Commission on the Holocaust, and be it further

RESOLVED, that the Rockland County Legislature hereby appoints Mrs. Georgine Hyde of Pomona and Dr. Harold Seigelbaum of West Nyack to be co-chairpersons of this Commission and Mr. Harold Reiss, RCC Adjunct Professor on the Holocaust, as member and Administrative Director to the Commission, and be it further

RESOLVED, that Dr. Seigelbaum, Mrs. Hyde and Mr. Reiss shall make recommendations within 60 days to the Rockland County Legislature as to the size and the full composition of the Commission, and be it further

RESOLVED, that the Rockland County Commission on the Holocaust shall make recommendations to the people and to the Legislature of Rockland County, on how to Commemorate and how to Memorialize this tragic period in Human History, and be it further

RESOLVED, that the Commission complete its work no later than by June, 1980.

CA/ajs
544061

The Legislature of Rockland County

County Office Building
New City, New York 10956

SAM COLMAN
Chairman

VICTORIA K. SEIGERMAN
Clerk

May 17, 1979

914-425-5000
914-425-5100

Mr. Harold Reiss
27 Smolley Drive
Monsey, New York

Re: Resolution No. 281 - Establishing a Rockland
County Commission on the Holocaust

Dear Mr. Reiss:

On behalf of the Legislature of Rockland County, I
would like to congratulate you on your appointment as a
member and Administrative Director to the Rockland County
Commission on the Holocaust.

I would appreciate your contacting Mr. August Hansen,
County Clerk, at your convenience, in order that you might
be duly sworn in as a member of this Commission.

Very truly yours,

Victoria K. Seigerman
Clerk to the Legislature

VKS:mu
Enc.
cc: Hon. Sam Colman
    Mr. August Hansen

26

Proclamation

Rockland County
State of New York

DAYS OF REMEMBRANCE OF
VICTIMS OF THE HOLOCAUST

April 13 and 14, 1980

WHEREAS, six million Jews and millions of other people were murdered in concentration camps as part of a program of extermination carried out by the Nazi party during World War II; and

WHEREAS, the people of the United States should recognize that all acts of bigotry are rooted in the cruelty of spirit and the callousness that led the Nazis to commit atrocities against millions of people, and should dedicate themselves to the principle of human equality; and

WHEREAS, the people of the United States should recognize that tyranny creates the political atmosphere in which bigotry flourishes, and should be vigilant to detect, and ready to resist, the tyrannical exercise of power; and

WHEREAS, on April 28 and 29 of 1945 the Armed Forces of the United States liberated the surviving victims of Nazi internment in the concentration camp in Dachau, Germany, and revealed to the world evidence of a tragic human holocaust that must never be forgotten; and

WHEREAS, the Nazi concentration camp in Dachau, Germany, is not only a shocking symbol of Nazi brutality and destruction, but also a symbol of the danger inherent in tyranny, the pernicious quality of bigotry, and the human capacity to be cruel.

NOW, THEREFORE, I, JOHN T. GRANT, Chairman of the Rockland County Legislature do hereby proclaim April 13 and 14, 1980, as DAYS OF REMEMBRANCE OF VICTIMS OF THE HOLOCAUST in the County of Rockland.

IN WITNESS WHEREOF, I have hereunto set my hand and caused the seal of the County of Rockland to be affixed this 7th day of April, 1980.

JOHN T. GRANT
Chairman of the Legislature

Victoria K. _____
Clerk to the Legislature
80-17
dh

27

The Legislature of Rockland County

Count Office Building
New City New York 10956

JOHN T. GRANT
Chairman
VICTORIA K. SEIGERMAN
Clerk

914-425-5000
914-425-5100

October 23, 1980

Mr. Harold Reiss
27 Smolley Drive
Monsey, New York 10952

Re: Resolution No. 706/80 - Appointment as
         Administrative Director to the Rockland
         County Holocaust Memorial Council

Dear Mr. Reiss:

On behalf of the Legislature of Rockland County, I would
like to congratulate you on your appointment as the
Administrative Director to the Rockland County Holocaust
Memorial Council.

I would appreciate your contacting Mr. Joseph Holland,
County Clerk, at your convenience, in order that you
might be duly sworn in as Director of this Council.

Very truly yours,

VICTORIA K. SEIGERMAN
Clerk to the Legislature

VKS:chb
enclosure

cc: Hon. John T. Grant
         Hon. Georgine Hyde
         Dr. Harold L. Siegelbaum
         Joseph Holland
         Charlotte Boyer

28

CHAPTER 2

CREATING A CENTER 1980-1982
The Holocaust Council
The Finkelstein Library
The Second Remembrance Day Program

In a memo dated June 13, 1980, that was circulated to all department heads of the Finkelstein Library, Sam Simon announced that a meeting would take place on July 10 at 2 PM in the library annex "regarding the proposed joint project between the Holocaust Committee and the Library." Copies of the memo were forwarded to the library's Board of Trustees, as well as to Dr. Siegelbaum, Mrs. Hyde, Mr. Reiss, and Mr. Josephs.

Exactly a month earlier, on May 13, 1980, the Clerk to the Legislature of Rockland County had sent the following memo to the Commission: "Attached herewith find a copy of Resolution no. 281 of 1979 which is self-explanatory. We wish to bring your particular attention to the last resolved clause that states: 'Resolved, that the Commission complete its work no later than by June, 1980.'"

On June 20, 1980, the date designated for the completion of the Commission's charge, Harry Reiss forwarded the Final Report of the Rockland County Commission of the Holocaust on behalf of the commission and its directors, Mrs. Georgine Hyde and Dr. Harold Siegelbaum. The report was divided into three subdivisions: (1) Development and Activities of the Commission, (2) Status of

Activities as of June, 1980, and (3) Recommendations. The recommendations included the disbanding of the Commission in favor of establishing a Rockland County Memorial Council and a privately funded Rockland Center for Holocaust Studies. The proposed center would be located initially at the Finkelstein Library in Spring Valley and would continue with the development of a suitable curriculum covering the Holocaust period for use in Rockland schools, both public and non-public. Another recommendation was to authorize a Holocaust Remembrance Day ceremony as an annual county event as a reminder to all citizens "of the need to maintain vigilance and dedication to democracy and liberty, to prevent such events from ever recurring." Resolution #5627 of the Rockland Legislature accepted these recommendations on October 21, 1980, and appointed Mrs. Georgine Hyde of Pomona and Dr. Harold Siegelbaum of West Nyack as Council co-chairpersons and Mr. Harry Reiss as Administrative Director. Two days later, the Clerk to the Legislature, Victoria Seigerman, sent letters to the three, congratulating them on their appointments and requesting that they contact County Clerk Joseph Holland to arrange for them to be duly sworn into office.

The members of the Commission were those who had been proposed originally: Rev. Robert Battles, Jr., Rev. Msg. James Cox, Dr. Seymour Eskow, Hon. Kenneth Gribetz, Hon. Georgine Hyde, Irving Kintisch, Hon. Brian Miele, Harry Reiss, Rabbi Paul Schuchalter, Dr. Harold Siegelbaum, Judge Morton Silberman, and Rabbi Dr. Moses Tendler. In addition, Hon. Sam Colman, Reverend Wilfred Findley, Leo Kelmar, Judge Bernard Stanger, and Bernard Weiner were added to the list. Mr. Kintisch later withdrew his name because he was moving out of the County. Official notices of the composition of the Commission were issued by then-Chairman of the Rockland County Legislature, John Grant. Now, by virtue of Rockland County Legislature Resolution #22, the Rockland

Holocaust Commission now became the Rockland County Holocaust Memorial Council.

The Council held its meetings over the next few months at the County Legislature's Law Library. On the agenda at the first full meeting, called for December 1, 1980, were the preparations of by-laws, filing for IRS tax-deductible status (501-03), filling of vacancies on the Council, the development of a curriculum for teaching the Holocaust, and plans for the second annual commemoration, designated for May 17, 1981. The Rockland Center for Holocaust Studies – library – museum – resource - was incorporated in January 1981, its location set at the Finkelstein Memorial Library.

At the same time, Harry Reiss was working with Dr. Sue Commanday of Rockland Community College to develop a curriculum "for use in 10th – grade history classes." The curriculum was ready by February 1981, at which time they submitted a grant request to the National Endowment for the Humanities (NEH) that covered not only a curriculum but also "teacher training conference and/or workshops, public events, guest lecturers for both school personnel and the general public." Commanday became Reiss's co-director of the project, which was called, "A Model for Collaboration between Community Agencies and Institutions in Developing Holocaust Study Programs."

The College agreed to submit the grant because of the efforts of its vice-president Philip Fey. In his opening statement requesting the NEH grant, Reiss reviewed the establishment of the National Commission of the Holocaust in November of 1978 and quoted from its report of May 1979: "The Holocaust radically challenges our understanding of morality, religion politics, government policy and of human nature itself. It is essential that Americans try to learn new models of behavior and responsibility in all aspects of national life…

There is a great deal of work yet to be done by all Americans." He continued: "An index of the amount of work needed can be taken from the recent signs that anti-Semitism is once more on the rise. Newspaper report many instances of synagogue defacement and desecration. Last week a large white swastika was painted in the parking lot of the Bais Yaakov High School of Spring Valley, New York, a school for Orthodox Jewish girls... Rockland County has one of the largest Jewish populations in the United States outside New York City, and this population has visible impact on the community's level of awareness of the Holocaust. Willingness has been expressed by a variety of community agencies and institutions to support this project on Holocaust study."

A board meeting of the Rockland Center for Holocaust Studies on May 19, 1981, with Herschel Greenbaum serving as temporary chair, unanimously passed a resolution that Dr. Harold Siegelbaum, Georgine Hyde, and Harry Reiss should be elected as President, Vice-President, and Executive Secretary of the Center, respectively. A second motion resolved that Harry Reiss should also serve as Executive Director of the organization. Dr. Siegelbaum asked Herschel Greenbaum to draw up a code of by-laws. The Board members voted in at this meeting were Dr. Harold Siegelbaum, Georgine Hyde, Harry Reiss, Kenneth Gribetz, Leo Kelmar, Fred Freitag, Rabbi Paul Schuchalter, Judge Bernard Stanger, Rabbi Moses Tendler, Bernard Weimer, Sam Colman, Rabbi Simon Potok, Jules, Stern, Rubin Josephs, Al Kirsch, Saul Kalish, Warren Berbit, Lou Kalus, Henry Zeisel, Joseph Warburg, Herschel Greenbaum, and Andrew Ackerman. Four names were later added: Anita Finkelstein, Rita Davis, Alex Morrow, and Alan Ritter.

During January and February 1981, the Remembrance Day Committee had already been at work planning the next Holocaust Commemoration. Congressman Benjamin Gilman, a member of the

Courtesy of The Journal News

Georgine Hyde, Harry Reiss and Leo Kelmar discuss Rockland County Holocaust Remembrance Day.

United States House of Representatives, was slated to be the keynote speaker at the event. In *The Journal News* of May 14, just three days prior to the Commemoration at Ramapo Senior High School, Harry Reiss declared: "The Jew has always been a weather vane of democracy. Holocaust Remembrance Day is our way of saying that if you don't worry about your neighbor's human rights, before you know it, someone will deny yours. That's how fragile democracy is... We want to avoid making Holocaust Remembrance Day only a media event. But at least in this country you are free to do that. In many countries you can't travel from town to town without passport identification." By 1981, six local synagogues had established annual Holocaust commemoration activities. Some felt that the Commission should sponsor the only program in the County, but Harry felt that it was a good thing to see Holocaust awareness spreading in other organizations, as well.

Mention was also made in this article about the close finalization of the plans to locate the new Center in the Finkelstein Memorial Library annex. Private fundraising was said to have raised about a quarter of the amount needed to proceed with the plans.

The program on May 17 was streamlined from the previous year. After the singing of the national anthem, three clergymen gave invocations: Rev. Monsignor James Cox, Minister Sidney Curry, and Rabbi Dr. Moses D. Tendler. John Grant, chairman of the Rockland County Legislature, presented a proclamation declaring Holocaust Remembrance Day. Rep. Benjamin Gilman, who was a well-known advocate of human rights, delivered the keynote address. His talk was followed by a showing of rare footage, a film generated by the Nazis themselves, of life in the Warsaw ghetto. This proved very potent for many survivors, who could remember the types of scenes portrayed. (The committee had debated showing the film after previewing it in the Reiss home. Despite the film's graphic views, the committee decided to present it because of the perceived need to preserve memory.) Indeed, it was felt afterwards that the footage was so effective that the committee decided to augment each subsequent program with some visual presentation, a component that continued for many years.

The national anthem was sung at this commemoration by Judy Siegelbaum, wife of the Holocaust Memorial Council's co-chair Dr. Harold Siegelbaum. For Orthodox Jews, this presented a problem. Not known in the larger community, and even among many non-Orthodox Jews, is a rabbinic law generally forbidding Jewish men to listen to a woman singing. Some Orthodox Jews now appealed to Harry Reiss not to have a woman sing. Harry faced a dilemma: he had the difficult task of explaining this issue to other Jews, who might find this concept strange and even offensive; on the other hand, always a gentle man, he wanted to avoid a confrontation and risk hurting anyone's feelings. Eventually he did make the issue known to Harold Siegelbaum, who was understandably amazed. Possibly in reaction to the stress of this issue, Harry contracted pneumonia before the program that year, and the matter was not resolved; in fact, it remained in limbo for two more years.

By the fourth year of the program, however, Harry had found a fortuitous solution. Coming out of the problems being presented to the committee each year by the Jewish War Veterans, who pressed to speak about their organization after the presentation of the colors, Harry invited a group of West Point cadets to present the colors that year. It turned out that West Point had a Jewish choir, which, if asked well in advance, would be pleased to go to Rockland County not only to sing the national anthem but also give a musical presentation. The West Point Jewish Choir was a featured attraction at the fourth Holocaust Remembrance Program.

CHAPTER 3

REACHING OUTWARD

Holocaust remembrance was taking root throughout the country, and the first World War Gathering of Survivors was held in Jerusalem in June. International travel was not commonplace for most Rockland County residents in 1981, and Harry Reiss was no exception. Still, he felt a burning desire to participate in this event, and so he made a reservation to fly to Israel to be part of the event as a press delegate. He also wanted to take with him tapes of survivors' testimonies from Rockland County. The week before his flight, he discussed his plans with a friend and neighbor, Dr. Becker, who had more flying experience. He pointed out that Harry's flight would not give him enough time to get to Jerusalem before Sabbath. Frantic calls to the travel agent were of no avail – there was no room on an earlier flight. Completely determined, Harry took his suitcase, went to the airport, declared himself "standby" and, with help from above, got a seat on the earlier plane, enabling him to arrive at his Jerusalem hotel before Sabbath. On the plane, Harry met many survivors. One woman from Los Angeles admitted: "I never spoke about the Holocaust until my grandchild said to me,

World Gathering
of Jewish
Holocaust Survivors

Opening Ceremony
Yad Vashem – Jerusalem
Monday, June 15, 1981

ADMIT ONE

№ 3387

'Grandma, why do you have your telephone number printed on your arm?'" On the bus ride to Jerusalem, the survivors sang songs of Israel and then of their old homelands. They asked the question: "Why me, why was I singled out [to survive]?"

Some 5,000 survivors and 1,000 second-generation survivors, the children of survivors, gathered at the first event of its kind. The second-generation children, who were in their 20's and 30's, asked one another: "How was it for you?" Harry recalled a children's memorial held outside the Knesset in the "golden light of pre-night Jerusalem," in his description. He sat next to Professor Gerald Draper, the former British Intelligence officer who had arrested and interrogated the commandant of Auschwitz, Rudolf Hoess. "When Draper spoke to Hoess about moral responsibilities and values," Harry later reported, "he received only a blank stare; when he discussed *logistics*, how difficult it must have been to move all those adults and children from all over Europe and get them into the camp [Auschwitz], and then dispose of them – Hoess became animated and voluble." The question came to Harry's mind; "Are we all members of the same human family?"

On his return, Harry summed up his reactions to the World Gathering in a letter titled, "Never Again," that appeared in *The Journal News* on August 1, 1981:

"When I returned to the United States, I tried to imagine how I would have felt had I been one of those who had been through that 'Kingdom of Hell.' Whatever my feelings might have been, in fact these survivors did not seek to avenge their wrongs through bloodshed. Instead, almost immediately upon their liberation, they began to rebuild their lives and families in many different countries. At the same time they continued to strive for justice in the world to prevent any recurrence of such horror." Referring to anti-Jewish incidents that had occurred in Rockland County that year, Harry spoke of the purpose of the Holocaust Center in Spring Valley, which was to "make available to citizens factual information on this tragic period... to help ensure that such events never happen again." Harry continued by quoting the words of Pastor Martin Niemoeller: First the Nazis went after Jews, but I wasn't a Jew, so I did not react. Then they went after the Catholics, so I didn't object. Then they went after trade workers, but I wasn't a trade worker, so I didn't stand up." Harry always stressed the need "for vigilance in defense of our democratic ideals."

It is interesting to note that in 2008, almost a year after Harry had died, Pastor Niemoeller's second wife and widow, Sybil Sarah Niemoeller, was the keynote speaker at the annual Holocaust Remembrance program in Rockland County. She announced to a rapt audience how she had converted to Judaism in 1990, hence, the addition of the middle name, "Sarah."

Harry, together with other Board members also attended the American Gathering of Jewish Holocaust survivors in Washington D.C. in 1983 and in Philadelphia in 1985.

Harry Reiss, Marc Berkowitz, Unidentified Participant, Dr. Zvi Nussbaum

During 1981, Harry Reiss, together with Georgine Hyde and Dr. Harold Siegelbaum, started bringing the idea of a Center to the community at large though a series of parlor meetings. It was felt necessary to explain to the public why it was important to teach what had happened in the Holocaust and to have a study center for Holocaust Studies for Jews and non-Jews alike. Harry had developed the rationale for this principle as early as 1979, giving expression to it at a UJA/Federation of Northern Westchester workshop in Mount Kisco that he led on April 22:

"I question the notion that the Holocaust period should be reserved for, and taught to, Jews exclusively. In this regard, some Jewish educators who feel that the Holocaust should be taught to either strengthen or create a Jewish identity among non-committed Jews, I believe, are also missing the mark. While the Holocaust has no doubt affected Jews more directly than other people, it also was, is, and should be taught as a major event in the history of the modern Western world. If the Holocaust is treated as such an event, we can then accept at least a possibility that many non-Jews may also be struggling with how to come to terms with what happened in the Holocaust period. As you probably know, many gentiles are interested in this period, and for a variety of reasons – legitimate and maybe not so pure. Modern German journalists, historians, and political analysts, for example, trace a direct connection between the lack of communication regarding the Holocaust on the part of German parents and grandparents and the rise of the various German urban terrorist organizations led by their children and grandchildren.

"So, if we accept the premise that the Holocaust was more than the catastrophe of the Jewish people; if we allow others to have a claim on it also – without any way taking away from the terrible, fearful role of the Jews in this event – we then move the

Holocaust into the wider human history area, and we can then stress in our presentation to school boards, administrators, and children, the brotherhood of all human experiences (good and bad, sublime and horrible) and the hope for creating a better world for all people.

"By universalizing the Holocaust period, then, we are saying, and most rightly, I believe, that, this material about the Holocaust must and will be taught because it covers a very important event in history. For non-Jews, teaching about the Holocaust will help to fill a major gap (in most cases) in their education. This was brought out to me most dramatically by the number of young adult non-Jews who have registered for the Holocaust course I give at RCC, and who stated that they had never realized that any such event had ever happened: and to correct misinformation acquired by Gentiles and Jews.

"On another level, knowledge of the Holocaust, how it developed, what happened, and the result, will enable everyone taking the course or unit to discuss implications of the Holocaust – implications having relevance to Jews and Gentiles alike – and to discuss these moral implications based on fact instead of emotion. I am speaking here about the moral questions which inevitably flow out of a study of the Holocaust – questions dealing with the relationship of God to man, of God to the Jewish people, of the nature of man, of divine law and human existence, of the historical as well as the moral and religious justification of the re-creation of Israel. All of these themes – so to speak – questions which are being taken seriously by non-Jewish theologians, historians and students of law, and which can and should be discussed in the classroom, appropriate to the grade level and experience of the children.

"One reason often given for teaching about the Holocaust is that we want to make sure that another Holocaust never happen. For after all, teaching about hate has never changed the extent of hatred in the world. A dream – a positive desire for peace, for ethical and moral living standards for all people – can however be a goal to be worked for by our children. This dream could become a major theme and reason for teaching the Holocaust; and it is also an appealing and positive reason for introducing Holocaust studies into a school curriculum, one that school boards can understand.

"Unfortunately, the trauma and the horrors of the Holocaust have in some instances made us as Jews withdraw into what we believe to be a self-protective shell, in a great and certainly valid mistrust of the Gentile world. But let us assume for a moment that that approach is the correct one, that anti-Semitism and hostile acts against Jews merely because they are Jews will always be with us. Does this mean that Jews and Gentiles cannot therefore get together to discuss the Holocaust and learn its lessons? One lesson – for example, the depths of depravity to which so-called civilized human beings can sink or the larger moral questions and implications of the Holocaust in the history of mankind – and then to work in some concentrated fashion to try to make a better world for the young people under our guidance? Think about this, because if as Jewish educators in public or non-public schools we cannot do this or at least attempt it, then we have to say, 'There is no hope for either the Jews or the world!'"

Harry refined his thoughts in a talk to a group of ASHAR Yeshiva parents, teachers, and others who gathered for a parlor meeting at the home of Dr. William and Debbie Schwartz in Monsey on January 18, 1981. It should be remembered that in 1981, the concept of Holocaust studies was new and untried. Many survivors were still reluctant to tell of their experiences; indeed, some regarded it as a secret to be kept from their children. This was the psychological climate of that time and formed the backdrop against which Harry spoke. For both harry Reiss and his audience, the subject had to be approached with both caution and courage.

In discussing the beginning of Holocaust denial and the fact that Europe was to all intents and purpose *judenrein* while Germany was a countervailing political force in Europe, Reiss stated:

The Rockland County
Holocaust Memorial Council
cordially invites you
to a
Coffee Hour Meeting
at the home of
Dr. and Mrs. William Schwartz
16 Smolley Drive
Monsey, New York
Sunday evening, the eighteenth of January
nineteen hundred and eighty-one
at nine o'clock.

R.S.V.P. 357-5333
425-4352

"But my friends, as Jews we can make sure that Hitler does not gain the ultimate victory – if we mean by that that Jews must be sure that evil and distortion are not allowed to spread. From the Holocaust to a great extent came Israel, and from the Holocaust experience have come tremendous questioning by Christians – that is, by non-Jews, as well as Jews – about the moral implications raised by the Holocaust experience…The hopeful tidings for us in all these conferences and books and causes is that the Holocaust is beginning to be recognized for what it was – a major event in history of the modern Western world. As such, please believe me when I tell you that many, many non-Jews of good will are struggling with how to come to terms with what happened in the Holocaust period. They want their children to understand this confrontation between good and absolute, methodical, planned, and executed evil. They are struggling with history curriculums in Germany and Britain and the United States of Austria, as to how to accurately present this event in the context of human history.

"As a teacher of Holocaust studies at Rockland Community College and as a parent of three children who are either in or have completed the ASHAR school, and as a history and political science teacher and supervisor for 20 years, and as an observant Jew, I have personally seen and had to deal with, in the public schools and with my children, the very sensitive and emotion-charged historical phenomena we call the Holocaust.

"There are a number of issues and questions in connection with the Holocaust that have to be addressed and it seems to me – that are not really usually adequately addressed by schools or parents. I hope to address some of these tonight – and I want your reactions to what I have to say in our discussion afterwards.

"To say that the Holocaust is of almost overwhelming significance to us as Jews is perhaps to state a truism that is also a cliché; but for those of us who were born during and after WWII – and so have received the information on the Holocaust once removed, as it were – many are not exactly sure as to the why it is significant today or as to the 'how' it should be transmitted to our own children, and even as to the whether or not it should be emphasized to Jewish young people in America.

"What I have just said I know may shock some of you, particularly those of you old enough to have lived through the years of the Holocaust from 1939-1945 or, God forbid, to have been a victim participant in these tragic events. To those of you in these categories, I must state now – that the emotional and personal trauma that you may experience when we talk about the Holocaust is not at all the way that your children – or their children view these events.

"So – the first question we have to ask ourselves as parents or teachers is 'Do we want our children to learn these horrible things that happened to the Jews in Europe?' How can recalling these atrocities serve any useful purpose to them in the present or future?

"I am aware, as Bob Salz wrote in his article, "Teaching the Holocaust," that one of our major goals in teaching our children about the Holocaust has been to try to instill in them 'a sense of identification with the Holocaust and thereby in some way strengthen their own sense of Jewish identity.' I believe that in this regard, we often try to place feelings of guilt or sorrow in children, who cannot really be expected to feel the loss of a third of their people in a six-year period, because they never knew what it was like to have them in the first place. So when we show them films or filmstrips of the Holocaust period, they may become emotionally aroused, but they may also react by refusing to engage in any further analytic thinking about these events."

Harry would often end his talks with a quote from Alexander Donat (*Out of the Whirlwind*): "To insist upon making the world uncomfortable with the memory of its guilt is a necessity for that moral reconstruction which may alone prevent a repetition of our Holocaust."

It should be remembered that in January 1981, there was as yet no Holocaust Memorial in New York City or Washington, D.C. A letter to *The New York Times* on November 21, 1980, written by Max Kalter, deplores this absence: "It is an unbelievable shame that 35 years after the end of World War I, no monument has been erected in the City of New York to honor the memory of the 6 million Jews killed by the Nazis during the Holocaust. My dear mother was gassed and burned in the ovens of Auschwitz on November 2, 1942. A long time ago, the city of N.Y. gave land for the erection of such a monument in Riverside Park at 83rd street. Since then, nothing has been done... The time is long overdue to erect a memorial worthy of the victims and worthy of New York City and its Great Jewish Community."

During the following year, various receptions continued to be held in private venues to spread the message of the Rockland Center for Holocaust Studies.

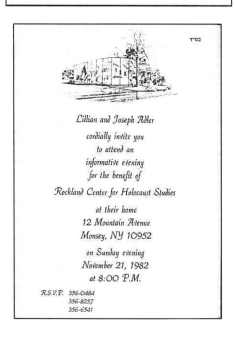

You are cordially invited to attend a coffee hour for the

Rockland Center for Holocaust Studies

at the home of

Dr. and Mrs. Harold L. Siegelbaum

259 Sickeltown Road

West Nyack, New York

on Thursday, September 4th, at 9 p.m.

R.S.V.P. — 914/357-5333
914/425-4352

A framework for the establishment of the Center
will be presented and discussed.

בס"ד

Lillian and Joseph Adler

cordially invite you
to attend an
informative evening
for the benefit of

Rockland Center for Holocaust Studies

at their home
12 Mountain Avenue
Monsey, NY 10952

on Sunday evening
November 21, 1982
at 8:00 P.M.

R.S.V.P. 356-0484
356-8257
356-6541

CHAPTER 4

REMEMBRANCES AND REALITIES - 1982-1984
The Inaugural Reception
First and Second Educators Conferences
Third, Fourth and Fifth Remembrance Programs

By March, 1981, the plans for locating the new Rockland County Holocaust Center in the annex to the Finkelstein Memorial Library in Spring Valley were being actively debated. Harry Reiss summed up final sticking points to settle, including who should carry the insurance for future exhibits, the library or the Center, and what would happen to the facilities of the Center should county interest abate and the Center would be forced to disband. The preliminary agreement which would be signed several months later in June, allowed for "A Holocaust Memorial Center to be constructed, operated, and maintained on the Library premises" with "the Center [paying] the cost of all construction necessary to house said Holocaust Memorial." It further allowed either party [to] terminate this agreement without cause upon 6 months notice to the other.

The preliminary agreement was signed several months later, in June, 1981. Present at the signing were Robert Finkelstein representing the library board, Sam Simon director of the library, Karl Hess, the architect charged with designing the renovations needed in the annex for the center; and representing the Center, Dr. Harold Siegelbaum, Georgine Hyde and Harry Reiss.

**Robert Finkelstein signing library agreement.
Harold Siegelbaum, Georgine Hyde looking in**

Courtesy of The Journal News

**Georgine Hyde, Robert Finkelstein, Dr. Harold
Siegelbaum, center, and Harry Reiss view
architect's model of proposed Holocaust
Center at Finkelstein Library**

It was ratified, as stated before, by the Library Board on October 29th of that year.

This preliminary agreement would be added to and modified as plans for rebuilding the annex by the Center were developed. The center was incorporated as a non-profit educational corporation under New York State Law on January 13, 1981 in a document drafted by Warren Berbit. It is interesting to note that the post office address listed in the incorporation paper was still 27 Smolley Drive, the home of Harry and Marion Reiss.

By the end of 1981, the financial goal of the proposed rebuilding of the annex was set at $250,000. With that goal in mind,

Sr. Rose Mary Thering
...people didn't care

the founders of the Center prepared their first fundraiser, an Inaugural Reception scheduled for Sunday, January 17, 1982, at Singer's Hotel in Spring Valley. The honoree was to be Samuel Weinberger, a Holocaust survivor and successful electrician in Rockland County. Mr. Weinberger had survived the war by hiding underground in Poland. The guest speaker was Sister Rose Thering, who was the director of secondary education at Seton Hall University and a vocal spokesperson regarding the role of the Catholic Church during and after the Holocaust. Sister Thering, in her letter accepting the invitation to speak, wrote: "I was truly moved by your invitation. I must confess I was a bit envious, since I would so much want someone to begin such a Center here at Seton Hall." Dr. Thering concluded her remarks at the reception by saying that "only constant reminders of the massacre of six million Jews in Nazi-controlled Europe can prevent a new Holocaust from occurring."

Mimi Kirsch was added to the board and joined her husband, Al Kirsch, in chairing the Reception. The event was financially

The pleasure of your company
is requested
at the
Inaugural Reception
for the
Rockland Center for Holocaust Studies

in tribute to
Samuel Weinberger

Guest Speaker
Sister Rose Thering, O.P., PH.D.
Director, Secondary Education, Seton Hall University

Sunday, the seventeenth of January
Nineteen hundred and eighty-two
at six-thirty in the evening
Viennese Table, Coffee and Liqueurs

Singer's Hotel
Central Avenue, Spring Valley, New York

Couvert $10.00 per person   *R.S.V.P.*

successful. Added to the $65,000 in pledges for the new Center was the sum of $25,000 pledged by Sam Weinberger. After the event, Reiss predicted that ground would be broken for the addition to the library annex by the spring. Other donations of various sums started to come in. Rose Hahn, president of the Yonatan Netanyahu Club of the Zionist Organization of America, presented a large collection of books and printed material to the newly planned Center. Gradually, the idea of renovating the existing annex transformed into the concept of rebuilding the annex completely. One of the catalysts for this thrust was Rubin Josephs, a survivor himself and successful builder in the county. Ruby, as he was called by everyone, brought a new dimension to the group. Aggressive, outspoken, and determined, he embarked on a fundraising campaign to achieve the goal of $250,000. When he was first introduced to Georgine Hyde and Marion Reiss, who were reviewing some material for a parlor program, he appeared almost like a "bull in a China shop." Nothing could stop him from raising the funds to build, he declared with a force that startled the two women, who were no slouches themselves in working for the new Center. It later turned out that he indeed let little stand in his way; he recounted tales of how he had withstood the entire Israeli police force to build a tennis center in Israel. He became a member of the Center's board in 1981. Other builders and architects slowly joined the original group, most notably Joseph Adler, another Holocaust survivor and builder, and Jacques Gerstenfeld, an architect. The latter joined architect Karl Hess, who had designed the renovations and who later became a trustee of the Center and eventually its president. The architectural plans changed several times, the original glass-fronted entrance morphing into more traditional siding, which was deemed more practical for the structure. One part of the original plan remained, however – the soaring roofline depicting hope and the future. The term "living memorial" to describe the Center was first used by Harry Reiss in an interview reported by Mitchell Weiss for

The Journal News on January 17, 1983. The term was later used by Museum of Jewish Heritage in Manhattan's Battery Park.

The Remembrance Day Committee had during this time been developing a pattern of its own. With its motto, "set aside an hour to remember," the committee set out each year to design a

Courtesy of The Jewish Week-American Examiner
L-R Sam Simon, Georgine Hyde, Harry Reiss, Ruby Josephs, Harold Siegelbaum, Robert Finkelstein

program that would last at most an hour and a quarter and a formula that would bring out hundreds of people each year on the designated Sunday afternoon at Ramapo Senior High School at precisely 2 PM. It proved to be a winning formula: First, there was the national anthem, followed by the presentation of the colors; then, in order, an invocation, an introduction by Harry Reiss, who was the chairman of the committee and of the program, next a keynote speaker, an audio-visual presentation, a candle-lighting ceremony, and a cantorial rendition of the Jewish memorial prayer.

The committee included a core of members, which was expanded or contracted each year. By 1982, the basic committee comprised Harry Reiss, Georgine Hyde, Harold Siegelbaum, Leo Kelmar, Saul and Janice Kalish, Marion Reiss, and Judge Bernard Stanger. Harry would sit on the piano bench or on a chair in front of the window of the Reiss living room and all the other members arranged themselves around the room, with the notable exception of Judge Stanger. He took a liking to the large club chair by the entrance to the room that was well lit by a lamp table, on which Marion was always careful to place a plate of the Judge's favorite nuts. Each meeting was an event, since everyone had the feeling that he or she was planning something extraordinary, and a fierce camaraderie resulted. In 1982, the original group was joined by Alex Morrow of Pomona, who was a neighbor of Miriam Morris and the owner of an envelope factory. He became the Center's main envelope donor, enabling large mailings of flyers for its events. Subsequently, however, he moved away and closed the envelope factory. Two new committee members that year were Edith Klein, who was a survivor from Berlin, and Barbara Grau, a former New York City school teacher colleague of Harry and a teacher at East Ramapo who came on board as the publicity chairperson of the annual event.

That year, too, the name of the organization was officially changed to the Rockland Center for Holocaust Studies, instead of the Rockland Council for Holocaust Studies. Its executive board also underwent a change, with Dr. Harold Siegelbaum becoming president and Georgine Hyde vice-president. Harry Reiss remained executive director, with the added title of executive secretary. A treasurer was added to the board, Alan Ritter.

The sense of purpose after the Inaugural Reception continued its momentum, and the fundraising goal seemed to be in sight. Not everyone agreed, however. Earlier, in a letter to the board dated October 13, 1981, Bernard Weiner expressed reservations about "placing the cart before the horse" i.e., fundraising for construction before setting down specifics of how the space would be used. His major concern seemed to be what was perceived as an escalation of building plans in excess of the existing annex space. Weiner also voiced the issue of available funds for paid employees, something that had not been financially possible. As a matter of fact, Harry Reiss had made a request for paid staff at the July meeting, but it was turned down for lack of funds.

Such reservations notwithstanding, a resolution, offered by Rubin Josephs and seconded by Rita Davis, was passed on February 4, 1982, authorizing the presentation of the building concept to the Finkelstein Library. At this meeting, Warren Berbit presented the IRS provisions to the board.

Throughout this entire period, the Center was reaching out to other institutions. For example, Judge Bernard Stanger had suggested at a board meeting on July 21, 1981, that county synagogues be involved through a kind of dues check-off participation system. Although the motion was carried unanimously by the trustees of the Center, it was never validated by the synagogues in question; and 25 years later, the proposal was still on the Center's agenda. The academic world was another focus of outreach. Harry Reiss reported at a board meeting on December 21, 1981, that he, Alex Morrow, and Leo Kelmar had met with officers of the Ramapo College (NJ) Holocaust Center and that Georgine Hyde had delivered an address there. Nearer to home, Rockland Community College participated in the early years of the creation of the Holocaust Center. RCC, of course, was the college where Harry Reiss had initiated his plea to teach a course about the Holocaust and where he had first expressed his vision to expand that education with commemoration of the Shoah (the Hebrew term for the Holocaust). Harry continued to teach the original Holocaust Studies course that he had developed there.

In the letter of endorsement that Rockland Community College vice-president Philip Fey had sent to the National Endowment of Humanities (NEH) when applying for a grant to establish its Holocaust program, he wrote: "Rockland Community College has an on-going interest and commitment to serving and educating populations within the region. The project to coordinate and implement a Holocaust studies program serves the interests and the needs of many within our County. This project will facilitate a

Educators' Conference at RCC

united effort by many of our local agencies in developing varied programs for school children, teachers, local groups, and others. Rockland Community College has offered a course on the Holocaust and will continue to do so. The college is also prepared to provide workshops and/or in-service training for secondary school teachers and others in the area of Holocaust curriculum training as long as there is interest." In fact, the college did sponsor one of the educational conferences that the Holocaust Center held at the college; the particular program was devoted to exploring the role of Italian Jews in the Holocaust.

The Survivors Group, organized originally as an advisory board to Rockland's Commission on the Holocaust, in particular bears mention. Chaired by Leo Kelmar, it was an autonomous group that comprised approximately 55 survivors of the European Holocaust. One of its first activities was to compile an extensive list of survivors living in the county. Its members would speak to various school and civic groups, providing first hand, factual accounts of their experiences. They were also involved in taping their experiences during World War II, and some of these tapes were used in the exhibits at the Center. Later, the Survivors Group started to organize a Children of Survivors group, which they felt had significant value in the larger context of the Holocaust tragedy.

By May 1981, the Center's board consisted of the following members: president – Dr. Harold Siegelbaum, vice-president – Georgine Hyde, executive director and secretary – Harry Reiss, trustees: Kenneth Gribetz, Leo Kelmar, Fred Freitag, Rabbi Paul Schuchalter, Rabbi Moses Tendler, Judge Bernard Stanger, Bernard Weiner, Sam Colman, Rabbi Simon Potok, Jules Stern, Rubin Josephs, Al Kirsch, Saul Kalish, Warren Berbit, Lou Kallus, Henry Zeisel, Joseph Warburg, Andrew Ackerman, and Herschel Greenbaum. Soon afterwards, Anita Finkelstein, Rita Davis, Alex Morrow and Alan Ritter were added to the list. Despite the prestigious assembly, Harold Siegelbaum wrote in a plaintive appeal, dated February 14, 1982, to the board: "Our meetings are usually attended by 10 out of our 26 Board members. We need increased participation by the Board members to help in our fund drive. There are members who have yet to attend a meeting." His plea was to be repeated time and again as the Center developed. Warren Berbit attempted to address this problem by proposing a resolution dropping trustees who were inactive. Such a resolution was also repeated from time to time in an attempt to ensure that trustees indeed formed a working board. Despite what Siegelbaum perceived to be poor attendance, the agendas of the meetings were so weighty that meetings seldom ended before 10:30 PM and were known to adjourn as late as 11:45 PM.

The focus of the meetings was more and more on fundraising. Many ideas, such as assessing synagogue members throughout the county, holding parlor meetings, and putting up donor plaques were suggested. In a note to board members on April 6, 1982, Harold Siegelbaum wrote: "At this stage we have lost the momentum generated from the Inaugural Reception. We need a chairperson to coordinate fund raising and get us moving." He also announced that the coming Remembrance Day program was to be held on April 25th.

The Holocaust Remembrance Day Program of 1982 featured Dr. Henry Feingold, author of *American Jewry during the Holocaust*, who charged that although American Jews did try to stop the killings, "there was no cohesiveness to the protest, and they were not listened to by the American leadership." After Feingold's keynote address, the film "Night in Fog" was shown, followed by a candle-lighting ceremony led by Georgine Hyde. Harry Reiss chaired the event for the third year in a row, and Dr. Siegelbaum provided the concluding remarks. The invocations were given by Monsignor James Cox and Rabbi Simon Potok. Kathryn Kahler of *The Journal News* wrote: "The darkness of history clouded Sunday's sunny weather for the nearly 300 people who gathered in Monsey to remember the 6 million Jews murdered during the Holocaust." The commemoration ceremony was taking root. For the next 16 years, whether in rain or sunny weather, from 500 to 800 people each year arrived slowly but inexorably for Holocaust Remembrance.

The Reiss family had particular reason to remember Feingold's visit. Stopping at the Reiss home before proceeding to Ramapo High School, the professor opened the front door a little too wide, allowing the Reiss cairn terrier, Tisi to make her escape into the park across the street. No one in the family had time to chase her, since she was a fast runner, and the dog remained missing overnight. What followed was a frantic search by foot, by radio announcement, and telephone. Eventually, a radio spot was picked up by a fellow dog lover, who recalled a friend picking up what was thought to be a lost dog. A happy family and dog were reunited the following evening after what must have been a wild adventure for Tisi. Professor Feingold was never told of this aftermath of his visit.

At the board meeting on May 20, 1982, the following officers were reelected: Harold Siegelbaum as president, Georgine Hyde as 1st vice-president, and Harry Reiss as executive director/secretary; a new office was instituted, 2nd vice-president, and Warren Berbit was elected to fill it. Mildred Zinn replaced Alan Ritter as Treasurer. Berbit had pointed out in his nominating committee report of May 11 that there should be clarification that the office of executive director was indeed an unpaid position. An Advisory Board was set up, and Lou Kallus and Alan Ritter were appointed to this new office. A motion, the first of many that evening, was passed to release from the Board of Trustees any member who missed three or more meetings. Joe Warburg accepted the position as chair of the fundraising committee. This committee joined the Survivor's committee, the Building committee, the Educational committee, and the Materials committee.

By September 9, 1982, most of the books donated by the Yonatan Netanyahu Club of the ZOA had been received, and the donation was noted by an appropriate bookplate. *The Journal News* reported on the first presentation of books from the ZOA at a ceremony held in the Annex of the Finkelstein Library on November 9, 1982. Mrs. Hahn of the ZOA explained as she presented the books that "young people, particularly, must be made aware of how and why the Holocaust was allowed to take place…[in order] to prevent the

Courtesy of The Journal News

Harry Reiss, left, Dr. Harold Siegelbaum, Karl Hess, Rose Hahn, Terry Levi and Samuel Simon, look over books and other printed material presented to the Rockland Center for the Holocaust

reoccurrence of such events in our country or anywhere in the world." Harry Reiss praised "two public agencies both cooperating to provide a new cultural resource at no cost to the public."

But fundraising was still going very slowly, with hardly half of the expected $250,000 needed to begin the building renovation raised as reported by the treasurer, Mildred Zinn, at the board meeting of October 21, 1982. Karl Hess had already completed a drawing for the Center. Donations, ads, and pledges at that point totaled approximately $110,000. Ruby Josephs and Bob Finkelstein, who were outlining plans for the Center, were ready to begin a new fundraising effort with a combined pledge of $200,000. A fundraising luncheon was scheduled to be held in December, with Orange and Rockland Utilities as sponsor and Rockland County Treasurer Joseph St. Lawrence, as guest speaker. The utilities company pledged a sum of $10,000 at the luncheon, which was subsequently held on December 10th. Mr. St. Lawrence, in recognizing the "tremendous need" for a Holocaust Study Center, donated the entire proceeds of a recently matured Israel Bond of approximately $1200 to the Center. At the October meeting, Leo Kelmar agreed to continue as president of the Survivors Committee. The first Educators Conference was also discussed, and the suggestion to send invitations to all teachers in the Rockland County School District was eventually carried out.

By bringing up "new business," Joseph Warburg read to the Board a letter from Rabbi Dr. Moses David Tendler, excerpted as follows: "You know I am strongly committed to the Holocaust Center project and will involve my congregation fully. However, I have one serious reservation. We have not discussed the need to be sensitive to the religious needs of the orthodox Jewish community. This sensitivity includes observance of Sabbath laws, Kashrut, as well as propriety of various fund raising functions..." Joseph Warburg then proposed a resolution, seconded by trustee Bernard Stanger, that

"The Rockland Center for Holocaust Studies and its Board, recognizing the need to be sensitive to the religious needs of the entire Jewish community, resolves that Sabbath laws, Kashrut (dietary laws), and continued propriety will be observed at all Center functions."

The motion passed unanimously, and this policy remained intact throughout the history of the Center. A copy of the resolution was sent to Rabbi Tendler by Harry Reiss as Executive Director on October 22, 1982.

At the January 6, 1983, meeting, Harry Reiss reported on the plans for the 4th Remembrance Day Commemoration, which was to take place on Sunday, April 10th, 1983. Harry and Warren Berbit also presented the need for additional clarification from the Finkelstein Library regarding its agreement on the groundbreaking ceremony. The last meeting with the Library Board had taken place on December 15, 1982, at which time there was a consensus regarding the close relationship of the two Boards. Robert Finkelstein, president of the Library Board, was also a member of the Center Board. In a letter he wrote to Harold Siegelbaum on December 17, 1982, Finkelstein agreed to the groundbreaking in January 1983, with the caveat that all publicity would have to be cleared by the library. He also specified that since the library was planning its own expansion and would retain an architect for that purpose, the architect would "consult and work closely with Mr. Hess, the Center's architect."

59

The groundbreaking ceremony for the new Holocaust Center building took place on January 17, 1983, a bitterly cold winter day in Spring Valley. Georgine Hyde, survivor of Auschwitz, spoke to the approximately

Courtesy of The Jewish Week-American Examiner

50 people who had arrived bundled up in their winter coats: "I remember when I stood in weather this cold without the trappings of shoes and coats. I don't know how I did it." Harry Reiss explained to the gathering that the Center's aims would be "threefold: to encourage the dissemination of educational materials dealing with the Holocaust, including teaching of the Holocaust studies in the public and private schools in the county; to have annual commemoration ceremonies and exhibits honoring the memory of those who perished in the Holocaust; and to house a museum, library, resource center, audio-visual material, and exhibits for use by students, educators and the public, free of charge." Holocaust survivors expressed their reasons

Courtesy of the Rockland County Times Rick Ferris ©

for being there. For Rubin Josephs, "it ensures that people will see what could happen if they are not on guard." Georgine Hyde recalled how difficult it was to speak of her experiences, but "I

L-R Rubin Josephs, chairman of the building committee; Dr. Harold Siegelbaum, chairman of the center; and Mrs. Bernard Golar, a member of the board of directors of the Finkelstein Memorial Library

realized that I owe it to the memory of those who did not survive to tell the world what happened to them."

While building plans were inching forward, subject to the never-ending need for raising funds, plans were underway for an Educator's Conference, the 4th Holocaust Remembrance Day Program, as well as for the Dedication and Remembrance Journal-Dinner. The Center Board scheduled an Educators Conference for March 22, 1983. The committee for the event was to be chaired by Bernie Weiner and included Georgine Hyde, Rita Davis, and Harry Reiss on the advisory committee. The plans included four workshops, a keynote speaker, the Reverend Bruce Bramlett, trustee of the Holocaust Center at Ramapo College, New Jersey, and rector of the St. Mark's Episcopal Church in Teaneck, New Jersey. The topic would be "Teaching about Genocide in Secondary Schools for Public and Private School Teachers." The program would be followed by a sit-down dinner for the educators, to be provided for by the Center and catered by RAM caterers. The location was to be the Holiday In in Nanuet, New York, and the hope was to continue such conferences in different venues for the next several years.

As planned, the 4th Remembrance Day Program took place on April 10, 1983. It was held at Ramapo Senior High School at 2 PM as the previous three programs have been, and only the weather presented a change of mood. Unlike the bright sunshine of the year before, April 10 this year was cold and rainy. In the words of *Journal News* reporter, Kevin McCoy, "Braving wind-whipped rain lighting candles, praying and singing songs, Rocklanders remembered the martyrs of the Holocaust Sunday and vowed such a massacre would never happen again." The planning committee worried that the weather would keep people away, but as in the past, the vast auditorium slowly and silently filled almost to capacity. The keynote speaker was William Donat, son of the famous Holocaust chronicler,

Alexander Donat. One of the few child survivors to be reunited with both parents after the war, Mr. Donat recalled how as a child of about five, he was reluctant to leave the convent where he had been hidden. His mother asked the nuns for a little time alone with him, during which she recalled his past affinity for good eating and promised him all kinds of delicacies if he would return with her. Fondly remembering the incident, Mr. Donat credited his felicitous appetite for the return to his family.

This fourth program marked the first time that the Jewish Cadet Choir of the West Point Military Academy performed at the

program. Harry had contacted Colonel Donald Bernstein, Deputy Post Commander at West Point and supervisor of the Chorus. The colonel made room in the choir's busy schedule to come to the Remembrance Day Program to present the Colors and to sing the Star Spangled Banner. This became the model for future years, as long as the date of the program did not interfere with the cadets' final examinations and other commitments.

The program led to an interesting experience for the Reiss family and to a relationship with Colonel Bernstein that lasted several years. Colonel and Mrs. Bernstein accompanied the cadets down to

Rockland County, and when they arrived an hour or so before the program was to begin, it was evident that they had not eaten lunch and were somewhat hungry. In the Reiss household there was a bit of a quandary. It was the day after Passover and the [chometz] larder was bare. Help came in the way of the local kosher pizza shop, which had opened for business as soon as allowed by Jewish law after Passover, and the Reisses ordered in boxes of kosher pizzas. To supplement these pizzas, Marion Reiss put out all the remaining boxes of matzo, along with tubs of butter and jam. Crowded around the kitchen table, the cadets together with the colonel and his wife declared the lunch "one of the best they had ever eaten." Good manners and politeness aside – after all, this was the U.S. Military Academy – another interesting insight was gained. Several of the cadets expressed surprise that matzo could be eaten at a regular meal. Their entire experience with matzo involved the Passover Seder, which was held regularly as a Jewish event at West Point. There followed a lively discussion between the cadets and the Reiss children about the delights of eating matzo at every meal on Passover and the different recipes they could be used in.

Colonel and Mrs. Bernstein returned to visit the Reiss home, and at Harry's invitation in his capacity as coordinator of the adult education program at the Community Synagogue of Monsey, the colonel was featured as a guest speaker at the Synagogue the following winter. The cadets also returned again over the next few years to participate in the Remembrance Day programs. One of Colonel Bernstein's proudest accomplishments at West Point was the building and opening of the West Point Jewish Chapel. Previously, Jewish cadets had to choose between the Protestant and Catholic venues for services. At the opening of the Jewish Chapel, the Reiss family met Rabbi and Mrs. Marc Abramowitz, who made sure that the kitchen at the new chapel would be kosher and who set the guidelines for its future use. Rabbi Abramowitz also became a friend of the Center and, like Colonel Bernstein, was invited by Harry to be a guest speaker at the Community Synagogue of Monsey.

On May 15, 1983, the Holocaust Center hosted a reception for Elie Wiesel in the Finkelstein Library's meeting room prior to his talk at Ramapo Senior High School. Wiesel's appearance also provided an opportunity for guests to view the site of the new Center. Enclosed with the copy of the invitation to Mr. Wiesel, Harry Reiss wrote on May 9, "At the reception, we will have a model of the proposed

The Rockland Center for Holocaust Studies
cordially invites you to attend
a Private Reception
for
Mr. Elie Wiesel
Sunday evening, May 15, 1983
at 6:30 p.m.
at The Finkelstein Library Annex Building
South Madison Avenue
Spring Valley, New York

For further information, call 357-5333 or 425-4352
No solicitation of funds

Mr. Wiesel will speak at Ramapo High School in Spring Valley at 8:00 p.m., under the sponsorship of The Rockland County Board of Rabbis.

Center building available, as well as an architectural rendering. We hope that at some point in your lecture you would mention our work, and the need for continued community support to help us in construction, preparation of exhibits and maintenance of the Rockland Center."

Elie Wiesel, members of Commission at Center

A new debate was fomenting among the Holocaust Center trustees. For the dual purposes of fundraising and a memorial, a marble memorial was proposed; it would feature the names of victims of the Holocaust, and its $20,000 cost would be offset by donations of $500 per name; an anticipated 1,000 names were hoped for. Many of the trustees, however, felt that the per-name donation would exclude victims of lesser means and, therefore, totally negated the concept of a wall memorial. It had been a tradition of the Center not to charge for any event or commemoration ceremony. So emotional did the May 1983 meeting become – it went until 11:15 PM – that the issue was tabled for June.

Before the June 1983 meeting, an open letter was circulated among Center trustees. Written by Warren Berbit, a trustee who had assisted with legal matters, the letter read, in part: "This concept [the wall] was presented to the board at the last meeting for the first time. Indeed, in the face of a large and, perhaps, unanticipated well-spring of opposition, some of which might have been fairly characterized as emotional to say the least, the matter was tabled. Although I think this need not be stated, discussions relating to the Holocaust most often contain an emotional component – no person with the slightest bit of compassion or heart can deal with this issue totally divorced from emotion…" Berbit then opined that paying a fee to memorialize those departed would "distort the purpose of the Center."

This letter was significant because it portended two recurring themes in the evolution of the organization. First was the fact that even small issues were likely to evoke emotional responses, sometimes out of proportion to the subject at hand. Those involved in the organization from the beginning and dedicated to its purposes became almost inured to this particular problem. However, on at least two occasions, new Board members recruited from the community resigned after a few meetings, citing the "emotionalism of the

65

meetings" as the cause. Secondly, the need to raise private funds to build and then maintain a Center and staff became an overriding issue, lasting to the present time.

In this instance, the meeting held on June 16, 1983, did not lack for attendance. Twenty trustees showed up, and the motion for the wall as presented was turned down. As in many of the Board's decisions, the denial of a serious proposal was somewhat mitigated by the formation of a committee to continue to study the subject, with the objective of recommending some modified version of a memorial wall.

The wall as such never materialized, but provisions were made for both memorial and honoree plaques to be purchased as a fundraising technique. The walls on which they were hung were located in inconspicuous places. Much later, memorial bricks, both indoor and outdoor, were sold. Looking down at the bricks or walking upon them, one could only wonder what the original trustees would have thought of the issue of dignity they had so fought over in their plans for memorializing loved ones.

As the building campaign intensified, a dichotomy developed between the drive for the new building and planning for the educational component of the Center. It became clear that the building committee needed legal empowerment to complete the actual construction plans. At a special meeting of the Board of Trustees in July of 1983 the following guidelines were suggested:

"The building committee is hereby authorized to negotiate a building contract for the Center with the bidder who, in the opinion of the Building Committee, results in the lowest price as balanced against obtaining good quality work on a reliable basis; and be it further resolved, that such contract shall be in a form as approved by the Center's Counsel and architect, and shall contain

66

at least the following terms and conditions as well as the ordinary terms and conditions:

1. No director or officer shall be personally liable.
2. Subject to approval of the State Education Department and the Trustees of the Library.
3. Shall state that no director or officer of the Center has any ties, whether directs or indirect, with the contractor.
4. If possible, shall be in two phases: the first phase for a completed shell at a cost not exceeding the current combined assets and pledges of the Center, and the second phase, exercisable at the will of the directors, being for completion of the interior.
5. Shall state that no liens or encumbrances may be placed against the real property of the library.

And be it further resolved that if the above conditions are met, the President of the Center, or in his absence the First Vice-President of the Center, is authorized to execute such contract in behalf of the Center."

At the September 16th Board meeting a resolution was moved by Bernard Stanger and seconded by Leo Kelmar was unanimously passed authorizing the Building committee, "to negotiate for the construction of the Center building at a budget of $190,000, and, with the authority of the building committee and approval of the president to go up an additional $10,000 if necessary."

As though to dispel any tensions between two objectives, the building construction and the educational mission, Harry Reiss reported at this meeting on the large meeting that had been held by the 2nd Generation Group and that it would be sending three representatives – Ms. Morris, Ms. Sternberg, and H. Karton – as liaisons with the Center.

In addition, a Journal Dinner, the first of many to be held for the purpose of raising funds, was planned, with Sam Colman as general chairman. Plans for the second Educator's Conference, to be held at Dominican College in Orangeburg, New York, and the next Remembrance Day commemoration were also aired at this time. It might be noted that the Center Board meetings were still being held in the Law Library of the Rockland County Office building in New City, New York.

Meanwhile, the library was completing its own expansion plans, and in December 1983, Robert Finkelstein indicated to the Center Board that eventually the entire Library annex building would be available for use by the Center. The Center's fundraising efforts, however, were proceeding slowly. Harold Siegelbaum had announced in November that Joe Adler, a local

Courtesy of The Journal News

Robert Finkelstein, left, and others in the fund drive review model of the proposed annex Sunday

builder and Holocaust survivor, had agreed to act as the personal contractor for the Center building and would work closely with Rubin Josephs, who chaired the building committee. The Center's architects, Jacques Gerstenfeld and Karl Hess, kept in touch with the library's architect, Willis Mills. Nevertheless, the library's director, Sam Simon, apparently wanted to keep a tight rein on developments. In a letter sent in March 1984, Simon emphasized the requirement that "all aspects of the proposed building for the center be seen and approved by [Mr. Mills]." This was reiterated by Robert Finkelstein in a letter dated May 31, 1984, to Dr. Siegelbaum that expressed the

Library Board's continuing concerns about the ongoing plans of the Center for its new building. Finkelstein wrote:

"Reflecting upon our meeting of May 16, 1984, the members of the Library Board are in general agreement as to the following:

1. The Library Board has a legal responsibility to the residents of the School District and inasmuch as the library is presently lacking adequate parking facilities, it is imperative that the facilities are not further decreased.
2. The building of the HMC [Holocaust Memorial Committee] will result in the displacement of some 10 parking spaces.
3. The representatives of the HMC acknowledged this problem and assured the Board that it will seek to offset this loss.
4. The architects for the HMC will prepare a working model for the Annex and an additional rendering of the proposed HMC so that the Library Board and its architect may study the compatibility of the two buildings."

The letter continued by outlining the mechanics of the relationships between the two entities:

"Since the proposed HMC will be built on Library property, it will generally be exempt from municipal ordinances. However, the Library Board will expect that the HMC will meet all comparable safety standards, e.g. fire retardant material, fire exits, smoke and fire detectors, and sprinkler system."

As if to underscore the still-developing rules for the new relationship, the letter expressed an unresolved issue in conflicting terms: First, "the Board expects to continue to use the Annex for library purposes [and] must be able to secure this part of the premises so that no entry may be gained from the HMC when the Annex is not in active use." And directly afterwards: "The HMC will have its own heating and air conditioning facility, and...will meter its own utilities." It concluded with a request for assistance with the upcoming bond vote, while assuring the Holocaust Center "that the [Library] Board intends to move ahead on the Center as rapidly as possible."

An article in *The Journal News* on April 26, 1984, summed up the diversity of the activities of the Rockland Holocaust Center at this time:

The Center's 5th annual Remembrance Day Program will be held on Sunday, April 29, 1984, at 2 PM at Ramapo High School, open to the public at no admission charge. This year's program entitled 'Righteousness and Resistance' honors the selfless work of Raoul Wallenberg, the Swedish diplomat who personally saved an estimated 300,000 people from Nazi slaughter in Budapest, Hungary during the summer and fall of 1944. Keynote speaker Mrs. Agnes Adachi was Wallenberg's chief lieutenant during his work in Budapest. Harry Reiss, the center's executive director and chairman of the Remembrance Day program will make the introductory remarks, a candle-lighting ceremony in memory of those who were murdered in the Holocaust will be led by Georgine Hyde, Vice-President of the center, Leo Kelmar of the Association of Holocaust Survivors of Rockland and Ann Katz, President of the Second Generation of Holocaust Survivors of Rockland County. For the second time the center is sponsoring a Rockland Educators Workshop Conference on May 2 from 3:30 to 8PM at Dominican College, Orangeburg. The center's extensive fundraising efforts will culminate with a county wide Book of Dedication and Remembrance Dinner on Sunday, June 10 at the Adolph Schreiber Hebrew Academy, Monsey. The Center's building scheduled for construction this year will be an addition to the annex building of the Finkelstein Memorial Library in Spring

Valley. It will house a museum-library resource center of factual materials dealing with the Holocaust, all available for use by students, teachers, and the general public at no charge.

At the 5th Remembrance Day Program, which honored the "righteous persons" who helped save Jews during the Holocaust, Harry Reiss spoke of "Raoul Wallenberg, [who] gave up his wealth, his social position and the safety of staying in Sweden to help save thousands and thousands of Jews in Hungary." On behalf of the Center, he presented an award to Monsignor Cox, stating: "But we are fortunate to have a number of righteous friends here in Rockland County and we are proud to honor a 'righteous friend' here, Monsignor James Cox, the Vicar of Rockland, as one of those who has shown concern and given support to the Center

Courtesy of Rockland Review

Harry Reiss presenting award to Monsignor Cox

for Holocaust studies from the beginning." To illustrate how Hitler's fanaticism had been directed pointedly at the Jewish people, Harry Reiss told of the experiences of a young Polish poet, Tad Borowski: "One day, Borowski met another Polish guard who told him about a new way that he had helped invent to exterminate Jews. 'You take four young boys with long hair and tie their hair together – then you light a match – drop it in their hair and watch the fire consume them.'" After this tale the events traditional candle-lighting ceremony took on added poignancy as a light for remembrance, not a fire for destruction. As in the past, all survivors in the audience were invited to light a candle, given out by members of the committee, and then Georgine Hyde summed up: "How do we remember those who wanted the free world to know and care about their fate? There were no prayers, no graves, no candles were lit in their memory, but they are not forgotten now or ever."

The candle-lighting ceremonies, so moving to all who participated in or witnessed them, were carried out without incident, since regular candles were distributed to whomever wished to light one. By the third Remembrance Day, the candles were wrapped in foil for the protection of the mostly elderly who lit and carried them. Later on, the regular candles were replaced by *yahrzeit*, or memorial candles in glasses, set up on a table for the people to light. At a much later date, the general lighting ceremony was replaced by the lighting of six symbolic candles by designated survivors. However, the raw power in those initial years of silent lines coming to the stage to light and hold a candle could not be replicated.

The 2nd Educator's Workshop Conference, co-sponsored by the Rockland Center and Dominican College, was held at the College on May 2, 1984. Titled "The Holocaust in Perspective," it featured as a keynote speaker Joseph Volker, Director of the Long Island Chapter of the National Conference of Christians and Jews. Breakout sessions were led by George Leahy of Nanuet High School; Harry Reiss, representing Rockland Community College; Melanie Stern, Anti-Defamation League; Joseph Cunneen, Mercy College; Rev. Dr. Robert Everett; and Rita Davis, Ramapo High School. Admission to the conference which included kosher dinner, cost $10.

The spirit of pure idealism and dedication to the mission of remembering and planning for future education was paramount even in the fundraising events of the iconic year, 1984. The *Journal of*

Dedication and Remembrance for the June 10, 1984, event was to be just that. The community at large was invited to place ads to memorialize loved ones or to make a statement about the horrors that had taken place. Although it was hoped that this would be a money-making project, commercial ads were hardly solicited and, when offered, were given a place in the back of the book. It was not unusual for an advertiser to request anonymity in the interests of undiluted memorial. The dinner was chaired by Assemblyman Sam Colman, who wrote that while the Holocaust was "uniquely Jewish because only Jews were elected to be killed, it also [has] universal significance because in it are encompassed all of history's massacres and tragedies… When we study the Holocaust, we learn how to spell NEVER AGAIN." Sam had been instrumental in securing the keynote speaker for the event, Congressman Sam Gejdenson of Connecticut.

Harry Reiss was the Journal coordinator and, responding to the desire of survivors to give permanent markers to their memories, he wrote in his forward: "A special leather-bound copy of this book will be permanently housed in the Center building, where the center itself will exist as an active, unique, and living memorial to those who lost their lives in the Holocaust." Several years after this dinner, Harry and Marion Reiss commissioned a white leather-bound copy of the Book of Remembrance, designed and crafted by Rabbi Chaim Spring, to be presented to the Center. It was displayed for a while in a locked glass case for reasons of safety, but this had the disadvantage of remaining open only to one page at a time. For a while, there was an attempt to tie it down to the front desk for visitors to peruse; in time, however, it was unfortunately designated to a secure cabinet in the secretary's office. One of the most vocal proponents of this book was Ilse Loeb, a survivor who had been hidden as a child. Unfortunately, Ilse was not present at the presentation of the Journal, but she eventually was instrumental in creating an exhibit of the

Hidden Children for the Center. It was an era of doing for the sake of the cause, and everyone was imbued with a sense of mission and selflessness.

The dinner committee consisted of Ilse Warburg, Marion Reiss, and Anita Finkelstein. Ilse and Marion spent many hours soliciting donations for flowers and favors. Even cases of soda were donated. It is interesting to note that in the present era of astronomical journal dinner prices and fundraising efforts by various organizations, the charge for attending the dinner was $37.50 per person. Still, the Journal of Remembrance brought it over $10,000. By June 1984, the assets of the Center, including pledges, amounted to about $250,000.

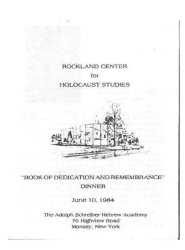

CHAPTER 5

DREAMERS AND BUILDERS, 1984-1986
Construction of the Center
The Sixth and Seventh Remembrance Day Programs
Third Educators Conference

Raising money for the building continued to be a major issue for the Center. Money came from private donors, from governmental agencies, and from corporations or other organizations, such as unions. One of the issues raised was the insistence by various unions on union labor for the building project, with accompanying rules of work and benefits. These demands raised costs, and the builders were concerned as to how to meet the budget. In the end it was decided that the Center would pay full union wages and benefits. However some of the unions showed their support for the work of the new Center both morally and financially. Particularly Cosmo Damiani, business manager of the International Brotherhood of Electrical Workers, and Bill Sopko, President of the Building and Trades Council of Rockland were instrumental in raising support for the Center. Both men were eventually recognized for their efforts on its behalf, Damiani in 1987, and Sopko in 1990. Damiani had declared his commitment to help raise money for the Center in a letter addressed to Harold Siegelbaum on June 10, 1984. He expressed regret at having missed attending the Journal of Remembrance Dinner and stated: "My commitment to you and Rubin [Josephs] still stands. I really do want to be involved because I think it [the Holocaust] is something that should be remembered. This place that we build should be the best for all to see and remember." He went on to request material to convey to those who might be interested in contributing.

A brochure had previously been prepared by the Center and was at this time distributed to residents of East Ramapo. Linda Winikow, then-State Senator, wrote to Harold Siegelbaum on June 13: "I was particularly pleased that one of my last accomplishments as a State Senator was the appropriation of $65,000 for the new Center." Winikow had left the Senate shortly before this letter to take a position as Vice-President of Orange and Rockland Utilities, where she continued to be a supporter of the Center. Thomas Griffin Jr., president and CEO of Orange and Rockland at the time, also sent a letter to express his regret at being out of town on the day of the dinner and to reiterate his company's support of the Center.

Almost exactly three years later, one June 28, 1987, Cosmo Damiani was honored by the Center at a special testimonial cocktail party held to recognize the fact that "Mr. Damiani and the IBEW are responsible for planning and completing all electrical work at the center. They donated all electrical fixtures and the labor to install those materials." In Mr. Damiani's own words: "I feel very strongly that this Center, which will be used by all the residents of Rockland and surrounding counties for research, study, and dissemination of information on that horrible time in history, is extremely important... [and] that everyone [may] be kept aware of what happened in the Holocaust so that it will never happen again."

It is interesting that this reception provided the lead article in the first Newsletter published by the Center, dated Summer 1987. In that same issue, a photo appeared of Thomas Griffin receiving a plaque in appreciation of his work on behalf of the Center. Although this is a leap ahead in the history of the center, it clearly illustrates the

Georgine Hyde, Sam Colman, Harry Reiss,
Joseph Adler, Cosmo Damiani

Thomas A. Griffin, Jr. (R) is presented
with a plaque in appreciation of his
efforts on behalf of the Rockland Center
for Holocaust Studies.

William A. Sopko, Rockland Union Leader, Honored

William A. Sopko, third from right, President of the Building
and Construction Trades Council of Rockland, is presented with
the Honor Award for his vital role in establishing and sustaining
the Rockland Center for Holocaust Studies. The presentation was
made at a cocktail party in his honor by Rubin Josephs, Center Board
Chairman (third from left). Looking on, left to right, are Paul Adler,
former Chairman of the Clarkstown Democratic Party; Bernard
Weiner, Managing Director; Anne Katz, Executive Vice President
and Al Kirsch, President of the Center.

growing and often overriding need to raise the necessary funds to actually build the Center – and the positive response from sometimes unexpected quarters.

Sometimes, the zeal for fundraising, however, overshadowed the inspirational and educational work which was going on at the center and which was indeed its raison d'etre. Even those most closely involved in the start-up of the Center fell into this trap. After the cocktail party honoring Cosmo Damiani in 1987, Sam Colman, who had spoken at the event, wrote the following letter to Harry Reiss and Georgine Hyde:

"Dear Georgine and Harry,

I owe both of you an apology when I misspoke today at the Holocaust Center Cocktail party. I called you both 'dreamers' who were at the very beginning of the Holocaust Center when it was only a dream. But you are both much more that dreamers – you are doers as well. I was trying to explain why both of you who started this dream were conspicuously unmentioned during the ceremonies. A better word for what I wanted to say is "educators." Today the ceremony was focusing on the builders but you, Georgine and Harry, are the master educators. Harry did as much as any one person [could do] to keep this whole project moving and ran every one of our Remembrance Days. Georgine, you were and still are our best contact with our educational communities. Please believe me when I called you "dreamers," I meant to associate you with the Holocaust Center when it was only a dream - the builders came later and helped you to implement the dream."

This dichotomy between builders and educators unfortunately continued through the opening of the new building. The word "founders" was often used as a synonym for builders, ignoring the inspiration and dream that had started and fueled the perpetuation of the memory of the Holocaust as represented by the Rockland Holocaust Center.

Much effort was necessarily put into developing materials to be used in fundraising. It should be noted that a good part of the early fundraising was devoted to collecting existing pledges. One of the first of these, a well-crafted, two-color flyer, dated August 1985, was meant to convey both the sense of fiscal urgency and the mission of the Center. It displayed three photos of the construction of the building, accompanied by this plea: "As the Center becomes a reality, the pledge you made to the center some time ago becomes even more important. The building is on the way to completion – we need you to pay your pledge now in order to finish the building – inside and outside… The Rockland Center's Officers and Board of Trustees have promised to make the Center a beacon of light and truth on the Holocaust period. Redeeming your pledge now will help insure that the center will be able to provide the programs, activities, and materials for these important goals." The appeal was signed by Joseph Adler, President of the Center; Harold Siegelbaum, Chairman of the Board; and Harry Reiss, Executive Director.

In a letter to the Board on January 7, 1985, Siegelbaum reported that construction of the new building had begun on December 19, 1984. He predicted completion by 1985, a goal that was not to be realized until 1988. He reviewed the two big successes of the year past, the Remembrance Day Program, with 500 in attendance, and the Educator's Conference at Dominican College, with 50 teachers participating. However, Siegelbaum still had to exhort Board members to attend meetings. Previously, Al Kirsch had proposed a step-down order of term of office for trustees, hoping for more continuity and a better flow of terms of offices, but his motion was not voted upon.

Rockland Center for Holocaust Studies, Inc.

P.O. Box 714 • Spring Valley, NY 10977
914 - 425-4352 • 914 - 357-5333

August 1985

Dear Friend:

These photos show the Rockland Center for Holocaust Studies building well along in the process of construction. We are targeting October of this year for completion of the exterior of the Center building.

As the Center becomes a reality, the pledge you made to the Center some time ago becomes even more important. The building is on the way to completion — we need you to pay your pledge now in order to finish the building — inside and outside. (If you haven't made a pledge yet, now is the time to do it.)

Recent events have served to emphasize the dangers to our democracy and freedom from terrorists and others who try to create a climate where a Holocaust situation could conceivably happen again.

The Rockland Center's Officers and Board of Trustees have promised to make the Center a beacon of light and truth on the Holocaust period. Redeeming your pledge now will help insure that the Center will be able to provide the programs, activities and materials for these important goals.

Sincerely,

Joseph Adler
President

Harold Siegelbaum, M.D.
Chairman of the Board

Harry Reiss
Executive Director

80

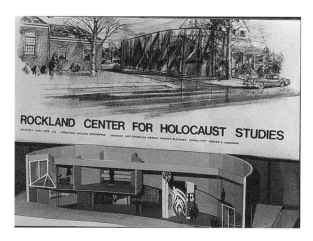

The Journal News, in an article written by Louis Lavell on December 26, 1984, described the commencement of the building of the Center:

"At the moment it's a dream, just a big hole in the ground outside a library in Spring Valley. In a few short months, though, the dream will be fulfilled with the opening of the Rockland County Holocaust Memorial Center. 'It's been a long time,' said Robert H. Finkelstein, president of Finkelstein Library, the county's largest. 'I'm very happy to see that they're doing it, and they're going ahead.' Projected to cost between $300,000 and $350,000 the Holocaust Center will be the first in the United States affiliated with a library, said Dr. Harold Siegelbaum, leader of the citizens' group. 'They had considered building the center at St. Thomas Aquinas College in Sparkhill or Rockland Community College in Viola. The organizers rejected St. Thomas because of Jewish opposition to locating a facility on Holocaust studies at a Catholic college. RCC was considered unsuitable for fear the center would lose its identity at a public institution.' Siegelbaum said that several hundred citizens contributed money toward the construction of the center. In addition to being used by county residents the organizers hope the center's resources will be used by teachers in the county's public and private schools as an aide in instruction. The center is an outgrowth of the Holocaust Commission created by the legislature five years ago. Members of the commission included Siegelbaum, Harry Reiss, the center's executive director, and Georgine Hyde, a member of the East Ramapo School Board. Joseph Adler of Monsey is general contractor for the project and Rubin Josephs of Monsey is chairman of the center's building committee."

It was not until May 1988, however, when Louis Lavelle would be able to write in another article: "After more than six years in the making, the Rockland Center for Holocaust Studies in Spring Valley is complete."

Meanwhile, on January 25 1985, Sandra Hendin writing in The Jewish Week, recognized the fact the "the fifth American Center dedicated to the memory of the Holocaust and the study of the destruction of East European Jewry is under construction in Spring Valley." Hendin captured the essence of the working relationship enjoyed by the Center's first triumvirate, Dr. Harold Siegelbaum, President; Georgine Hyde, Vice President; and Harry Reiss, Executive Director:

"We are a unique operation," said Executive Director Harry Reiss, who initiated the project in 1977 when he persuaded the Israel and Judaic Studies Department of the Rockland Community College to teach a course about the Holocaust. Although still awaiting a home of its own, the center has been active for the past two years encouraging the teaching of the Holocaust in Rockland County's schools and holding seminars for teachers. The center has also conducted yearly Holocaust commemorative ceremonies, according to Harold Siegelbaum, Center president. The four-level building, Siegelbaum explained, will house a museum, library, resource center and permanent memorial. The main level will serve as an exhibition room for permanent and rotating exhibits. The lower floor will house a multimedia facility. On the mezzanine level will be the resource center, and the top floor will provide more space for research and study, as well as room for lectures and large programs. Half of the building's estimated $500,000 construction cost has been raised through private contributions. Reiss expects future funds to be raised through membership dues, private grants, and financial support from the county's congregations. The establishment of the center comes at a time of increasing interest in the history of the Holocaust, said

Georgine Hyde, Center vice-president. The young people in our classrooms are eager to know about the work that was destroyed, she said. While the cause of human rights, dignity and justice came too late for the victims of the Holocaust, their scattered ashes and unmarked graves inspired this idea."

In just a few quotes from each of the founders, this article summed up the Center's past, present, and hopes for the future.

Meanwhile, the Board was continuing to plan future events and to install new members. Francis Sternberg and Miriam Morris of the Second Generation Group joined the Board of Trustees at the February 1985 meeting. At this meeting, it was also decided that the outgoing president would become chairman of the Board. This step was designed to provide a continuity of leadership for the expanding Board. By the time of the installation of the new Board in June, Al Kirsch's motion of a three-tier Board of 3, 2, and 1year members had been put into place. Composing the new Board elected in June 1985 were these members:

President, Joseph Adler; Chairman of the Board, Harold Siegelbaum; Vice Presidents, Warren Berbit, Georgine Hyde, and Anita Finkelstein; Executive-Director/Secretary, Harry Reiss; Treasurer, Mildred Zinn.

The 3-year trustees were Joseph Adler, Harold Siegelbaum, Warren Berbit, Georgine Hyde, Harry Reiss, Anita Finkelstein, Mildred Zinn, Norman Bleckner, Rubin Josephs, Al Kirsch, ;and Mimi Kirsch.

The 2-year trustees were Andrew Ackerman, Rita Davis, Robert Finkelstein, Jacques Gerstenfeld, Saul Kalish, Alexander Morrow, Bernard Stanger, Sam Weinberger, Bernard Weiner, and Joseph Warburg.

The 1-year trustees were Samuel Colman, Evelyn Daks, Fred Freitag, Laurence Gordon, Karl Hess, Ilse Loeb, Isadore Schlachter, Morris Schwartz, Fran Sternberg, and Henry Zeisel.

A Board of Governors was established, consisting of Rabbi Louis Frishman, Kenneth Gribetz, Leo Kelmar, Rabbi Simon Potok, Rabbi Paul Schuchalter, Israel Stern, and Rabbi Dr. Moses Tendler.

This pattern was preserved although the exact terms of office never seemed to keep up to date. Indeed, as late as 2009, the Nominating Committee for the Board was grappling with the graduated terms of office. As for the Board of Governors, although the hope was that it would take an active part in fundraising, it never gained the momentum of the actual Board of Trustees.

Plans for the 6th annual Holocaust Remembrance program, scheduled for April 28, 1985, focused on honoring the liberators of the death camps, as the event coincided with the 40th anniversary of the Allied victory in Europe. The program itself included a panel discussion by four of the liberators who lived in Rockland County. Speaking about their experiences were Morton Baron, former Supervisor of the Town of Ramapo; Isadore Schlachter, William Derevensky, and Morris Schwartz. In reporting on the discussion in *The Journal News*, Jerry DeMarco quoted Derevensky, who recalled that he and his fellow soldiers found "30 or 40 open railroad cars full of bodies, some still alive yet." Baron described finding "the furnaces [that] were still going." Schlachter, Director of the Orangeburg Library, remembered that "the smell was terrible and it remains with me today."

The four veterans did not hesitate to comment on the political event of the day, President Reagan's planned visit to Germany to commemorate the 40th anniversary of the end of World War II and to visit the military cemetery at Bitburg, where former S.S. soldiers were among the buried. The Journal News reported on this and continued: "Harry Reiss, executive director of the Rockland Center for Holocaust Studies, agreed with those who maintain that today's Germans were not responsible for the execution of million Jews and others 'but neither should this generation be free of the need to know and understand what happened then, so that it will never happen again.'" But Morris Schwarz disagreed: "The greater number of Germans who are living today [and who]were teen-agers or adults [then] were collaborators, they cheered every victory." Isadore Schlachter, with a prescience of what became the mantra for the dying generation of Holocaust survivors and witnesses, said: I think we look back after 40 years because many of us will not be here in another 10 or 20 or 30 or 40 years. Perhaps this is the last time some of us can give testimony of what we saw or what we did."

Although the program included the moving candle-lighting ceremony led by Georgine Hyde and accompanied by Cantor David Rosenzweig of the Jewish Community Center in Spring Valley, members of the Remembrance Day planning committee later felt that the panel format had diluted the remembrance part of the program, the climax of which was the address of the keynote speaker.

The Bitburg trip, however, remained in the forefront of controversy in the county. In a speech at the Nyack Library on April 14, Harry Reiss expressed the hope that during Reagan's planned visit to Germany, the president would mention the millions who perished under the Nazis. "It is a truism that if we deny history, we open the door to abuses or our own liberty," Reiss warned. In responding to protests form Jewish groups across the country and from the American Legion about President Reagan's planned trip, a spokesman for the President later said that the President was considering a "balancing event," such as a visit to a synagogue.

Nine years later, Harry Reiss was to experience the situation himself, when he attended a conference on anti-Semitism in Berlin in 1994. The conference was sponsored by Von Humboldt University, where Albert Einstein had once taught. Reiss found incidents of desecrations of Jewish cemeteries. But he also found hope. Harry recalled in an article written by Steve Lieberman on April 18, 1994, in *The Journal News*: "The night after I left, about 5,000 people came out on the streets of Berlin holding candles against the violence." Reiss continued: "Overall Berlin is very safe. Jews who are left there are very much like the invisible people. I asked, where are the Jewish spots? and somebody told me about a little Jewish café a few blocks away from the Oranienburg Synagogue. Every place where there are Jews, there are police. I looked for the Jewish Community Center. The address number was 11, and I couldn't find the building between numbers 10 and 12. I asked store owners and they said nothing or didn't understand me. I found it in a courtyard hidden from the public. If you didn't know where to look, you couldn't find it. You had to buzz an intercom to get in. There were security cameras, guards. The Jews who were there didn't see anything strange in all this."

By late 1985, the Center had raised funds beyond its original goal of $250,000, and the Center's treasurer, Mildred Zinn, reported an equity of $275,000, with about $70,000 in pledges outstanding. Against the equity, the building had already cost more than $200,000, with the permanent exhibit still to be contracted and installed. Norman Blechner, an interior designer, had come on board by this time and was preparing an interior concept. It was still hoped that the Center could be opened by the Spring of 1986. Again, this optimism was quite shy of the actual opening date.

At the Board Meeting on November 21, 1985, the Educators Task Force described plans for the next Educator's Conference, which was planned for December 4th. Since a meal would be provided to the teachers who attended, the question was raised as to whether these meals would be kosher, since the event would be held this time in a different venue. Judge Bernard Stanger moved that all food served under the auspices of the Center, no matter where an event was held, would adhere to the Jewish laws of kashruth. This policy was adopted unanimously and has remained in force to the present time. Another policy adopted at this meeting was in regard to taking out ads in journals of other organizations. At the time, Ruby Josephs was being honored by the Monsey Jewish Center, and some Board members felt the Center should acknowledge this through a congratulatory ad in that synagogue's publication. After some discussion, it was decided that rather than have the Center itself send money to other organizations, a committee called the "Friends of the Rockland Center for Holocaust Studies" would place the ad, with the funds to this end to be raised privately; this was done by Al Kirsch, Harry Reiss, and Mildred Zinn.

The third Educator's Conference, titled "Teaching the Holocaust – Ethical and Moral Concerns," co-sponsored by BOCES and the Rockland Center for Holocaust Studies, turned out to be a very successful event. Held at the Tappan Zee Towne house (since closed) in Nyack, New York, it featured Sister Rose Thering as the keynote speaker. The event cost the Center a little over $2000, including an honorarium for the speaker and a light supper for the participants. The conference, though, saw the emergence of a recurring theme for the Center. In accordance with the recently adopted policy, the meals served were kosher; however, a tension existed between those who resented this policy and those who were dedicated to upholding it. The costs of these conferences had always been a concern, going back to 1983, when a letter, dated April 19, 1983, sent from the then-conference chair, Bernard Weiner, stated in a response to a request for a refund from someone who could not attend: "The caterer had to be paid for every dinner ordered – consequently no refunds could be forthcoming."

Excerpts from correspondence with Harry Reiss illustrate how emotions could run high on many issues, even among close co-workers. In a letter addressed to "Dear Harry", one of his colleagues wrote: "I wish to apologize for hanging up on you. However, for personal reasons I have a short fuse and don't have the patience to argue and argue the same points. At an initial meeting, the Superintendent of BOCES said he would take care financially of all expenses except food. I said I will handle this. You forget and chose to remember what suits you. As far as catering glatt kosher meals, the board originally gave $500 and then increased it to $1000. We are cash poor and considerable thought should be given to how monies are expended. If you wish to write a rebuttal, OK."

A rebuttal was forthcoming. "We have been working together and in general agreement for over 6 years and I hope we will continue for many years to come. But it was with great sorrow and regret that I received and read your letter. Since I value your continued friendship, I am complying with your request to respond in writing. The concept of maintaining kashruth laws for all food service in which the Center is involved became part of the by-laws of the Center in 1982-83. The decision was made and voted on at that time, not to please any one person, but rather as a matter of principle considering the nature of the organization. As such the discussion is viewed by me as a matter of policy, not as an individual matter of my view versus someone else's. Since I have handled the arrangements for the educators' conference to date, I assumed I would be doing the same for the December conference this year. In any case I completely believe that we are motivated by the same concerns to see that all the goals of the center are fulfilled and that the Rockland Center for

Holocaust Studies will be a model for other Holocaust Centers to follow. With best regards, Harry."

Alan Weissberg, director of Secondary Education for the East Ramapo School District, wrote to Harry Reiss: "Dear Harry. The December 4, 1985, 3rd Educators Conference *Teaching the Holocaust: Ethical and Moral Concerns* was a resounding success. As Executive Director for the Rockland Center for Holocaust Studies, you have played a major role in the ongoing development of this project. Your dedication, interest, concern and knowledge helped to provide a most positive direction. You also served as a presenter in the Roundtable. I thought your comments were important and very well received by all in attendance. In addition you took care of the food arrangements and everything turned out exceptionally well. Harry, it is always a pleasure working with you."

That "everything turned out well" was a testimony to the dedication of many of the original committee, especially Georgine Hyde, who wrote to Siegelbaum on September 14, 1985: "Dear Harold, I am sorry it will not be possible for me to attend the 9/19 meeting [re: Educators Conference]. Sometimes I think there must an easier way to bring it all about. Well, we have moved the mountains before! With a bit of luck and lots of work and patience, we may do it again. So many various temperaments – it takes a lot out of me! Thanks for Alan Weissberg. Love, Georgine."

Mountains were indeed moved, for this conference and then again for other conferences in the years to come. In histories of other Holocaust centers and museums, both those that came before and those that came after the Rockland Center, it was evident that an additional emotional overlay always characterized the Holocaust-related entity.

One area of the new building was set aside for a museum, but the purchase of artifacts for it proved to be expensive. Inquires about a Torah scroll from the Czech Memorial Trust – to take one example – brought the response that a permanent loan of this artifact would cost $600. Trustees were also beginning to consider hiring a professional curator to prepare the permanent exhibit, which would entail further expenses. Meanwhile, donations of artifacts were being received and reviewed from time to time. Andy Ackerman, who worked at the Jewish Museum in Manhattan, offered his help in this endeavor. A gift of $5000 from Arco Management in Suffern was especially welcome at that point.

It was at the last meeting in 1985, in December, that Siegelbaum introduced the topic of hiring a paid employee to coordinate the Center's activities, which up to this point had been coordinated by himself as president and Harry Reiss as Executive Director. Reiss expressed his willingness to continue to work without pay, but recognized that, with the new construction, there was need for someone to be available and responsible on site. The Board thought that a salary of about $200 a week might be offered, and a committee was formed to draw up a job description. One month later, at the January 30 1986, meeting, it was decided to hire Ms. Esther Pal as coordinator of the Center, but on a month-to-month basis. One of her first duties involved the coordination and computerization of all names of donors and pledges. Along with her appointment, it was also decided that Ms. Pal would need the services of a computer expert, at a maximum rate of $8 per hour, to handle programs that had already been purchased.

Members of the Board were encouraged to view Holocaust museums in other parts of the country. Early in January 1986, Harry Reiss and Norman Blechner visited the Detroit Holocaust Memorial Center. They were very impressed with the exhibitions, which were coordinated there by Deby Lebow, who offered to come to advise Rockland's facility. Most impressive at the Detroit exhibit were video testimonies of survivors and slide footage of different events of the Holocaust. The Rockland representatives were told that 80% of the visitors to the Detroit Center were non-Jews. After they reported back to the board, the Center's new president, Joe Adler, expressed the hope that the Rockland Center would have equal success in attracting people of all religions to its exhibits. Harold Siegelbaum had visited a Holocaust center in Phoenix, Arizona, and presented his observations that that institution was able to function on a full volunteer contingent, composed mainly of senior citizens. Some time after this meeting, Joe Adler visited the Dallas, Texas, Holocaust Center, which had a railway car and a memorial room. The operating budget there, he related, was $100,000 a year. It was clear that major fundraising would be needed here, as well.

Preparation of the exhibits took on a note of urgency as the completion of the Center building was progressing. It was decided that the Second Generation Group would continue its project of videotaping survivors, with the goal of having these tapes become part of the future permanent exhibition. But fundraising for all these projects was paramount. Ruby Josephs suggested going to public entities and agencies, such as the National Endowment for the Humanities, and applying for grant monies. Indeed, on application to the Village of Spring Valley, funding was allocated to the Center for building an access ramp for handicapped persons.

The concept of training volunteers was put into action by a Center Trustee, Fran Sternberg, who was working with Brenda Greenberg, coordinator of volunteer activities at RSVP (Retired Senior Volunteer Program.) The task was to organize and train volunteers for all jobs, as well as docents for the museum exhibits when ready. It is interesting to note that 25 years later, Brenda

Greenberg was trying to reactivate the volunteer program, which had fallen into disuse.

The next Holocaust Remembrance Program, planned for early Spring 1986, was to be devoted to the Vanished Civilization, destroyed by the Nazis. A follow-up Educator's Conference at BOCES was also planned, as was a second Journal Dinner.

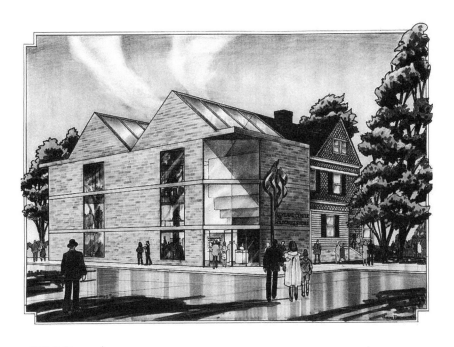

94

CHAPTER 6

COMPLETION OF THE CENTER BUILDING
Seventh and Eighth Remembrance Programs
Fourth Educators Conference
Opening of the Center

By the March 1986 Board meeting, it was formally decided to hire Deby Lebow of Detroit to put together the permanent exhibit for the Center. Norman Blechner pointed out that the Center, when completed, would have even more exhibition and meeting space that did either the Detroit or the Dallas facility. In August 1986, Ms. Lebow presented an invoice to the Center totaling $2488.22 for eight renderings and a blueprint.

The 7th Annual Holocaust Remembrance Day Commemoration took place on May 4th, 1986. As in previous years, the audience filled the Ramapo Senior High School auditorium to remember. This year's topic was the "Vanished Jewish Communities," and the keynote speaker was introduced as follows: "The Europe the Jews helped build up was destroyed within four years. We're talking about nine million Jews; we're talking about writers, artists, little towns, shtetls, big cities from the Atlantic to the Urals. Out of nine

Courtesy of Jewish Tribune

95

million, six million are dead by 1945. The figures are there, but did Hitler wipe out the spirit of the Jews?" Yale Strom, klezmer musician, photographer, and journalist, was the featured speaker. He spoke of his travels in Europe, talking to and filming the remaining Jews. His message was that a vital remnant of Jewish life still existed there, perhaps to be reborn. He would later publish a book about his experiences.

Seven years after the first Rockland County Holocaust Commemoration program in 1980, a new phenomenon was observed in the county. Individual organizations and synagogues were beginning to hold their own memorial programs on Yom HaShoah, Holocaust Day. Many of those associated with the RCHS considered this an infringement on what had become the major county-wide event. Harry Reiss, however, took an entirely different approach. In introducing the program on May 4th, he made the following statement: "When we began in 1980 with the first Remembrance Day program, there was not one such program in Rockland. Today, almost every Jewish organization has a Remembrance Day program. For that we are proud. In 1977, when I gave a course on the Holocaust at Rockland Community College, there was not another such course in the county. Today, every one of the eight school districts in the county has a course on the Holocaust." Unlike those who saw these individual memorial programs as competition, Reiss did not view it as a matter of concern; for him this was a sign of success!

In June 1986, a nominating committee for the following year was set up under the chairmanship of Warren Berbit. The committee consisted of Joe Adler, Georgine Hyde, Karl Hess, Harold Siegelbaum, Al Kirsch, Fran Sternberg, and Mildred Zinn. It was the first time that Harry Reiss was not on the committee. He had just undertaken to coordinate a panel on "Holocaust Education in

College" at RCC, and so he could be excused from one committee. In any event, he served as chair of the Dinner-Journal committee.

Two significant changes emerged from that committee meeting of July 10, 1986. Mildred Zinn resigned as treasurer, and Esther Pal's title was reconfigured as Managing Director. Harry Reiss, who had been the executive director from the very beginning of the Center, found himself in the ambiguous position of being one of two "directors." Eventually, Reiss's title was changed to executive secretary. However, it was the ideal of creating the Center as a tool for education about the Holocaust that had motivated Harry, and he continued to work toward that goal in many capacities for 21 more years, until his death.

Along with Reiss's new title and position, Monte Melamud took over the post of treasurer. At the October 28, 1986, meeting, Esther Pal announced her resignation, but she was invited to join the Board of Trustees. A search committee was formed, but it was decided even before the meeting ended to hire Fran Sternberg to take over the position being vacated.

The Journal Dinner being planned would honor Dr. Harold Siegelbaum, who in 1986 held the position of Chairman of the Board. The event was held at Singer's in Spring Valley, on August 24, 1986. The flyleaf of the invitation echoed the need for financial support as follows: "At this moment, the exterior is virtually completed. The Center now needs funds to complete the interior and provide for future activities and maintenance."

Deby Lebow, as mentioned, had submitted several versions of a museum narrative for the main exhibition space, and a special meeting was called for November 11th to consider them. A committee consisting of Fran Sternberg, Harry Reiss, Georgine Hyde, Andy Ackerman, and Bernard Weiner was formed to supervise the

97

development of the design chosen. Norman Blechner announced that he would design the display cases and other appurtenances and that his firm would charge close to cost price for the work. It was not until the end of the year, however, that the Board finalized a contract with Ms. Lebow for the exhibit.

Money continued to be a major concern. The Center's president, Joe Adler, proposed collecting membership dues with a graduated-fee scale based on several levels of giving and that this income should compose the major portion of the Center's budget. (The proposed scale: regular member - $18, contributor - $25, sponsor - $50, friend - $100, donor - $250, and patron - $500.) The Center's operating budget was estimated to be about $75,000 a year, and this figure did not include its capital budget. When the treasurer drew up the budget, the actual total expenditure for 1986 was listed as $117,402. Total assets were listed as $402,828; after contractual obligations for construction and the exhibition were taken into account, the Center was left with a liability of $240,000. The exhibit itself was budgeted at $97,000; later, the total cost of the exhibition would be estimated at about $175,000. Ruby Josephs and Al Kirsch stressed the need for fundraisers and private donations. Anita Finkelstein showed the board the prototype of a "tribute card" that members could purchase for a minimum of $5. Still another expense at this time was the Center's first Newsletter, which had a target publication date of January 1987.

By early 1987, the Board was still waiting for a visit by Ms. Lebow to present a plan for the exhibit. The next Remembrance Day program was being planned, with Terrence Des Pres, a professor at Colgate University and author of the acclaimed *The Survivor – An Anatomy of Life in the Death Camps* as the keynote speaker. This was the first year that more than a token honorarium would be paid. The speaker's fee was $1000, necessitating a motion of approval by the Board. Previously, costs had been kept to a minimum by volunteer publicity efforts, especially by various synagogues and organizations in the county.

All members of the board were invited to join the planning committee, which also consisted of non-Board members. The committee that year consisted of Esther Clifford, Barbara Grau, Georgine Hyde, Janice and Saul Kalish, Anne Katz, Ilse Loeb, Ed Krupnik, Harry Reiss, Harold Siegelbaum, Judge Bernard Stanger, Len Spiegel, and Fran Sternberg, with Harry as chairman. A discussion arose at a Board meeting as to the propriety of distributing membership materials at the Remembrance Day program. It is interesting that the ideal of having no commercial of political connection whatsoever in the program was so ingrained in the committee's formula for this event that the planning committee members on the board overwhelmingly opposed the proposal so as not to dilute the pure memorial nature of the event. However, a compromise suggested by Joseph Adler was adopted, which was that brochures would be unobtrusively displayed on a table in the lobby and so be available to anyone who wished to take one. Eventually that became the practice, with volunteer members of the committee manning the table.

On Sunday, April 26, 1987, at precisely 2 PM, the eighth Remembrance Day program began. Harry Reiss declared the topic: "This will be a living memorial." Rabbi Henry Sosland gave the invocation, and Miriam Morris presented a slide display of her father's Holocaust paintings. Professor Des Pres, who was not Jewish, described how he became interested in the topic after realizing that very little research had been done up to that time about the survivors themselves. Feeling that their stories might be lost to posterity, he began to interview them himself and found than many "survived the horrors of the Nazi extermination camps by maintaining their dignity and humanity, often by helping others." His address was all the more moving in the light of both his scholarship and his sincere empathy for the victims and survivors. Sadly enough, later that year, Des Pres was found dead in his home in a situation termed accidental. The Center, truly affected by this loss, sent a letter of condolence to his family.

The Remembrance Day program was concluded, as always, with the rendition of the liturgical "Kel Maleh Rachamim" (God of Mercy) prayer by Cantor Rosenzweig and the lighting of the memorial candles. That year, the survivors were joined not only by the Second Generation but also by their grandchildren in a solemn but somehow uplifting ceremony. After the program ended, the audience slowly filed out, but members of the planning remained to take down the huge posters that  they had put up hours before and to store them for another year. Coming right after Passover each year, the annual commemoration had indeed become part of the calendar of the Rockland community.

Business as usual returned in May, with an emphasis on raising the money to open the Center. Cash on hand was reported as $57,584; pledges and grants pending totaled $77,588, for a total accounts receivable of $135,112. The projected expenditures, including contractual agreements and outstanding bills, amounted to $210,949.91. It was little surprise that fundraising became a major part of the organizational agenda and continued to be so for the coming decades. It is worth noting that governmental pledges from the Town of Ramapo ($2,500), the Village of Spring Valley ($15,000), U.S. Congressman Benjamin Gilman ($1,000), New York State Senator Gene Levy ($5,000), and New York State Assemblyman Sam Colman ($5,000) constituted the major commitments outstanding. Nonetheless, as the building of the Center was going forward, an Educators' Conference was again planned for the Fall. It was expected, however, that the BOCES would fund a large portion of the teacher workshops scheduled for that event. This was in fact confirmed at the Board meeting in June by Georgine Hyde, who was then Chairperson of the east Ramapo School Board.

At the June meeting, building committee chairman Ruby Josephs reported that the Center was about $100,000 short of the funds needed for the completion of the building itself and for the final budget of the exhibitions. Not included among these expenses were the captions for the exhibitions, which were developed free of charge from a script prepared by the archivist Sybil Milton, director of the archives of the Leo Baeck Institute in New York City, and approved by the Center's editorial committee, chaired by Harry Reiss. The new slate of officers and trustees was also presented in June: President – Joseph Adler; Chairman of the board – Dr. Harold Siegelbaum; Vice Presidents – Rubin Josephs, Al Kirsch, and Dorothy Steinmetz; Executive Secretary – Harry Reiss; Treasurer – Monte Melamed. The three-tier trustees list was finally in place: one year – Lillian Adler, Evelyn Daks, Percy Goldstein, Anne Katz, Phillip Marcus, Jack Schloss, Morris Schwartz, and Jeffrey Troodler; two year – Andrew Ackerman, Esther Clifford, Rita Davis, Anita Finkelstein, Jacques Gerstenfeld, Karl Hess, Charlotte Klarfeld, Bernard Stanger, Joseph Warburg, and Henry Zeisel; three year – Warren Berbit, Norman Bleckner, Robert Finkelstein, Georgine Hyde, Ilse Loeb, Mimi Kirsch, Esther Pal, Sam Simon, Sam Weinberger, and Bernard Weiner. A mantra was introduced here by Mimi Kirsch, to be repeated often over the coming decades, reminding trustees that an absence of more than three meetings would result in the termination of office. Attendance at the June meeting was a high of 18.

The death of Dr. Harold Siegelbaum between the June and July meeting in 1987, after his active fighting of his illness for some time, was a blow if not a shock to the board of the Holocaust Center. He had become involved in the center from the beginning as a service to the community, and both he and his wife, Judy, had become dedicated to Holocaust Remembrance as a unique cause. His death was a personal loss to both Harry Reiss and Marion, who had come to value his invaluable interaction and also his personal friendship. Moments of silence were observed by the Board in Dr. Siegelbaum's memory, a tradition that unfortunately was to be repeated time and again in the future of the Center. In his memory, Board member Warren Berbitt composed a poem, a poignant line being: "I vow to remember and speak." The Board decided that a plaque would be put up indicating that the building was dedicated in the memory of Harold Siegelbaum, one of the Center's three original founders, but that the name of the Center would remain unchanged. It was also decided at this time that a plaque bearing the names of all of the charter members would be installed in the center of the building. Two additional trustees were also voted in: Mrs. Judy Siegelbaum and Mr. Martin Goldstein. At the request of the Center's president, Joe Adler, an amendment to the Center's by-laws was offered. The amendment, in the form of a resolution drawn up by Warren Berbit, stated: "...the officers of the Center shall comprise the Executive Committee, chaired by the president, which committee shall have authority relating to the day to day operations of the center in accordance with the policies of the board of Trustees; which authority shall include giving direction to the Managing Director." The motion was passed unanimously.

To commemorate Dr. Siegelbaum's contribution to the building of the Center, John Lang, a friend of the deceased, sent out a letter requesting donors to become benefactors of the Harold Siegelbaum Memorial Lecture Series for the Holocaust Center with a minimum sponsorship of $500. Within several months of the letter, more than $17,000 was raised from among Harold Siegelbaum's family, continues to provide a source of revenue for the Center to the present time.

In August 1987, the Center's Managing Director, Fran Sternberg, had tendered her resignation, stating personal and familial obligations as the reason for her leaving. She urged the Board to set up a reasonable set of guidelines for the job description when seeking future applicants.

The building and exhibit costs were constantly rising, so that it was necessary at the September meeting to vote an increase to $50,000 to enable Deby Lebow and associates to complete their work for the museum. The total construction cost for the new facility was now approaching $200,000. To keep up with the expenses, the Center was forced to borrow $25,000.

It is interesting to note that at this time, the New York City Museum's "A Living Memorial to the Holocaust – Museum of Jewish Heritage" was in the process of culminating plans to build its museum and collecting artifacts for its permanent collection. It would be almost ten years later, though, that this museum finally opened its doors.

The 4th Educators' Conference on Teaching the Holocaust was held on December 8th at the Tappan Zee Inn in Nyack. It was hoped that the event, still co-sponsored by BOCES, would attract participation from more diverse areas. BOCES was now paying for all costs, including publicity, facilities, teaching materials, and speakers' honorariums. The Center paid for the light supper provided to the participants. The meal this year was catered by Bagels and More of Monsey.

The raw memories of the survivors came to the fore once again during the ninth Holocaust Remembrance Day program, held as always on a Sunday afternoon in April, this time on April 24, 1988, at Ramapo Senior High School. Although the program was titled, "The Survivor and the State of Israel," the guest speaker, Leon Wells, himself a death camp survivor and, in his own recounting, one of those inmates assigned to retrieve gold fillings from the dead and then burn their bodies, was the author of *The Death Brigade*. His talk stressed the experiences of those in the death camp and those in Poland who had survived. He told of escaping from an order of death by blending in with another group and later being assigned to a work detail that had him essentially, in his words, "looking for my own body."

Courtesy of The Journal News

Leon Wells addresses group yesterday at the ninth annual Rockland County Holocaust Remembrance Day program at Ramapo High School in Spring Valley

In his introduction, Harry Reiss quoted form Wells's book. When he arrived in the Janowska labor camp, Wells observed the capos "shoot a woman, and the woman's child is sitting next to her in a pool of blood with her head on her dead mother's breast, sleeping. An SS man wakes the child by whipping her. She must go with the other children to the sands [a place for mass murder]. The child screams in terror and faints. The child gets up and starts to run and an SS man goes after her. The child yells and the murderer decides to shoot her on the spot." Eventually Wells, who lost seven brothers and sisters in the death camps, escaped from Janowska and was hidden by a non-Jewish farmer. He claimed that 90% of the Jews who survived the war in Poland did so because "of the kindness of Catholic Poles and Ukrainians." This remark evoked several audience responses objecting to his labeling the Polish people as heroes, since most of the killing was done in their midst. He evoked further outcries from his listeners later on in his talk when he claimed that "no one ever heard anyone crying "Shema Israel" when locked in the gas chambers.

The powerful emotional reactions of the audience to Wells comments were attested to by Georgine Hyde: "This is the ninth year I have been here [the Remembrance program] and it's always difficult to go back to these memories: but it is very important to those who can't be with us – those who died. Those innocent human beings who suffered and died in such a horrible manner have to be enshrined in in our hearts forever." One member of the audience expressed his emotion graphically: "He [Leon Wells] went through nothing compared to what I went through," the man said, lifting up his sleeve to show the concentration camp numbers branded on his wrist. A second-generation member expressed his feelings at the ceremony: "The Holocaust is something that is never out of my thoughts; but is very special to me each year. I do it [i.e., attend the program] each time to honor my parents, who were both survivors. And I bring my children so that it will remain in their memory, too," he explained as he embraced his children, who represented the third-generation group.

Indeed, the candle-lighting ceremony led by Georgine Hyde included not only the Second Generation group but their children, as well, the third generation! Cantor Rosenzweig's rendition of the Kel Maleh Rachamim prayer brought the audience, now standing for the candle lighting, to tears.

A reporter for the *Rockland Review* commented on "the large number of young people in the audience." Harry Reiss concluded: "Nine years ago when we first started this program, there were very few commemorations in the county. Now there are more and more remembrances being held. It seems that we opened the door to what has become a major event, and interest is probably at an all time high."

That November, the Holocaust Center held its first Kristallnacht Commemoration in the Center building. In the words of Harry Reiss, who moderated the program, "Kristallnacht shattered freedoms and showed the world that a government would no longer protect people, protect civil rights and guarantee law and order." Three survivors of that fateful night recalled their experiences. Edith Kling, who was 9 years old at the time, recalled that Jews were rounded up and taken to a riverbank, "where they would be spat on and have garbage dumped on them by hordes standing on nearby bridges." She and her family eventually escaped because her father, a Polish national, was given asylum by the Polish consulate. Esther Clifford, who lost both of her parents and a brother and sister in the Holocaust, disobeyed Nazi orders on Kristallnacht and ran away. She recalled: "People were so busy throwing stones, they didn't even notice me. The glass was crushing under my shoes while I was running." Eric Block remembered firemen standing idly outside a burning synagogue in his native Munich. Reiss ended the program by noting that "indifference and inertia are as much the villain as bigotry."

Later on, Ilse Loeb, chairperson of the Survivors Group, recalled being sent to Holland from Vienna after Kristallnacht. She was hidden by several non-Jewish families and survived the war, but her parents never made it to Holland and were killed in an extermination camp.

The end of December 1987 saw the payment of several outstanding bills – to the Post Office, to Bagels and More and to Sybil Milton as an honorarium for consultation services. Dr. Milton had volunteered her expertise in reviewing the proposed order of exhibits for the Center.

By the first meeting of the Center Board in January 1988, Bernard Weiner was confirmed as Managing Director of the Center. The new Executive Board was listed as follows: Chairman – Joseph Adler; President – Rubin Josephs; Vice Presidents – Al Kirsch, Dorothy Steinmetz, and Frances Sternberg; Executive Secretary – Harry Reiss; Treasurer – Monte Melamed. There was some discussion about changing the status of the Center to a Museum; however, on the advice of lawyers, who said that the process would take over a year and a half, the motion was tabled for further investigation.

Plans for the Spring were outlined in February: the Remembrance Day Program would be held on April 24th and the opening of the new building was scheduled for May 15th. Anne Katz was elected to chair the latter program, which would feature a breakfast, speakers, and tours of the new building. The keynote speaker was Rabbi Irving Greenberg, who had been active in many Holocaust events and whom Reiss knew form Holocaust conferences in Philadelphia. Rabbi Greenberg, president and co-founder of the National Learning Center for Jewish Leadership, turned out to be a most effective keynote speaker. In 2011, Rabbi Greenberg would again address the Holocaust Center at a dinner marking its thirty year history of commemoration and education.

The ceremony for the opening of the Rockland Center for Holocaust Studies finally took place, as planned, on a beautiful, sunny day, May 15, 1988. The parking lot of the Finkelstein Library, adjacent to the new Holocaust Center Building, provided the venue for the auspicious event. Rabbi Irving Greenberg noted in his address that there were then fewer than 25 such centers throughout the United States. The Jewish Tribune of New York noted that May 15, 1988, was the 45th anniversary of the blowing up of the Warsaw Ghetto in 1943, and the 21st anniversary, according to the Jewish calendar (the 28th of Iyar, 5727) of the liberation and reunification of Jerusalem. Inside the Center were exhibited original art works by David Friedman, a Holocaust survivor who had died in 1980; the exhibit had been mounted by his daughter, Miriam Morris. Many of these works would later be hung at Yad Vashem and other museums. In viewing the main museum exhibit, located on the new building's lower floor, one survivor exclaimed: "It's like seeing your life come back again." Another commented: "People see it but can't believe it."

More than 500 people attended the opening. The program included and invocation by Rabbi Dr. Moses Tendler and an benediction by Rabbi Paul Schuchalter. Extending greetings were the Center's President, Rubin Josephs; Chairman of the Board, Joseph Adler; Founder and Executive Secretary, Harry

Courtesy of The Journal News
Hundreds gathered at the opening of the Rockland Center for Holocaust Studies on the anniversary of the crushing of the Warsaw Ghetto. It is estimated that there are only 25 such Centers in the world.

Reiss; Founder and Trustee, Georgine Hyde; Managing Director, Bernard Wiener; President of the Second Generation Group, Anne Katz; President of the Finkelstein Library, Robert Finkelstein; and President of Orange and Rockland Utilities, Thomas Griffin. Musical renditions were given by Cantor Harold Rifkin and by the ASHAR Children's Choir.

Harry Reiss addressed the topic of the "History of the Center." Following are his remarks:

"After ten years of planning and perseverance, the Center today opens its door to you. Ten years ago, 1978, there were very few people in the county or elsewhere who had any strong feelings about establishing any memorial concerning the European Holocaust. As an instructor at Rockland Community College, when I suggested teaching a course on the Holocaust, it was given a very marginal chance of succeeding. But some people in the nation and in the county did care – including our State Assemblyman (then-County Legislator), Sam Colman. With his help, on May 15, 1979, exactly nine years ago, the Rockland County Commission on the Holocaust was created, with Dr. Harold Siegelbaum, Georgine Hyde, and myself to get it started and establish its priorities.

"What we decided then are still the priorities for the Center: (1) education of our young people so that such tragic events will never be allowed to happen again; (2) commemoration and remembrance of the six million who were murdered; and (3) establishment of a vibrant resource and study center that would be a beacon of light for the entire county and Lower Hudson region. Since then, we have held nine annual Remembrance programs and four Educators Conferences. Two years later, in 1981, the commission evolved into today's Rockland Center for Holocaust Studies. That same year, the Center signed a unique, cooperative agreement with the Finkelstein Library that resulted in the Center building being constructed on the library's grounds.

"Standing here today and recounting some of the Center's history recalled to mind what a *Journal News* reporter wrote on November 22, 1979. [And I quote:] "Reiss said that he can envision a day sometime in the future when a County Memorial to the Holocaust will be dedicated. There would be thousands of people there, committed to keeping the memory of the Holocaust alive, in the hope that it would never happen again. 'That would be quite a day,' he said." To update what I said nine years ago, this **is** quite a day! Thank You."

The new building's opening came exactly 10 years, 1 month, and 2 days after the publication in The Journal News on April 13, 1978, of the article, "Teacher Stresses Lessons of the Past," which described Harry Reiss's vision in regard to the Holocaust: "You can react to the Holocaust in one of three ways: you can deny it ever happened, you can say forget about it, or you can bear witness because it did happen and you must see that it doesn't happen again.:

Bearing witness, teaching, and remembering so that the evils of history would not be repeated became the work of the Holocaust Center, and it continues to this day.

**Rockland Center
for Holocaust Studies**

Dedication Program
Sunday, May 15, 1988

THE ROCKLAND CENTER FOR HOLOCAUST STUDIES
Spring Valley, New York
MAY 15, 1988, 10:00 A.M.
Dedication Ceremony

Al Kirsch, *Master of Ceremonies*

Invocation............................ Rabbi Dr. Moses Tendler, *Community Synagogue of Monsey*
Welcome... Rubin Josephs, *President, R.C.H.S.*
History of Center........................... Harry Reiss, *Founder and Executive Secretary, R.C.H.S.*
Survivors' Legacy.................................... Georgine Hyde, *Founder and Trustee, R.C.H.S.*
Musical Selection .... Cantor Harold Rifkin, *New City Jewish Center*
Center Rationale.................................... Joseph Adler, *Chairman of the Board, R.C.H.S.*
Keynote Address .... Rabbi Irving Greenberg, *President and Co-Founder of CLAL: The
National Jewish Center for Learning and Leadership*
Library Greetings .... Robert Finkelstein, *President of the Board of Trustees, Finkelstein Memorial Library*
Educational Programs .... Bernard Weiner, *Managing Director, R.C.H.S.*
Second Generation Legacy .... Anne Katz, *Founder and Past President
Second Generation of Rockland County*
Musical Selection .... Children's Choir, *Adolph Schreiber Hebrew Academy*
Dedication Plaque .... Thomas A. Griffin, Jr., *President and Chief Operating Officer
Orange and Rockland Utilities*
Benediction........................ Rabbi Paul Schuchalter, *Congregation Sons of Israel, Suffern*

111

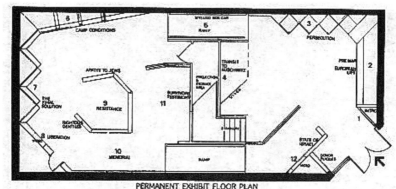

PERMANENT EXHIBIT FLOOR PLAN

A GUIDE TO THE PERMANENT EXHIBIT

The permanent exhibit is a two-story museum that combines graphics, photo-montages, artifacts, and audio-visual displays to detail every phase of the Holocaust.

1. INTRODUCTION AND DEDICATION: "This Center is dedicated to those who perished in the Holocaust."
2. PRE-WAR EUROPEAN LIFE evokes the vitality and breadth of pre-war European Jewry, its culture and society.
3. PERSECUTION chronicles Hitler's anti-Semitic campaigns, and the initial persecution and ghettoization of the Jews.
4. Through the use of audio-visual techniques, TRANSIT TO AUSCHWITZ depicts the magnitude of the deportation of European Jewry to the death camps in the East.
5. The RAMP, which resembles a BOX CAR, leads down into the darkness, to the second part of the exhibit.
6. CAMP CONDITIONS describes the sufferings of prisoners of the concentration camps.
7. The horror of Hitler's mass murder of European Jewry is detailed in the "Final Solution."
8. LIBERATION is a video presentation of documentary film footage of the Allies entering a concentration camp.
9. This section consists of the Jewish RESISTANCE to the Nazis, the RIGHTEOUS GENTILES who risked their lives to rescue Jews and the WORLD'S RESPONSE of apathy and indifference to the plight of European Jewry.
10. Twelve engraved granite MEMORIAL PLAQUES testify to the grievous loss of Jewish lives in the major concentration camps.
11. The SURVIVORS THEATER provides the testimony of local survivors of the Holocaust as they bear witness to their sufferings and the fates of their loved ones and communities.
12. A second RAMP leads back to the light. The final panels of the exhibit celebrate the courage of the survivors who rebuilt their lives in America and other countries. The last videotape depicts the triumph of the establishment of the STATE OF ISRAEL.

THE ROCKLAND CENTER FOR HOLOCAUST STUDIES

BUILDING COMMITTEE
Rubin Josephs, Chairman
Joseph Adler - Al Kirsch

EXHIBIT FABRICATION AND DESIGN COORDINATOR
Norman Bleckner

MUSEUM AND EXHIBIT DESIGN
Deby Lebow Design Associates
Southfield, Michigan

ARCHITECTS
Jacques H. Gerstenfeld, A.I.A.
Karl Hess, A.I.A.

FABRICATION AND INSTALLATION OF MUSEUM EXHIBITS
ExhibitGroup New York

THE ROCKLAND CENTER FOR HOLOCAUST STUDIES GRATEFULLY
ACKNOWLEDGES THE SERVICES AND/OR PERMISSIONS PROVIDED
BY THE FOLLOWING COMPANIES AND/OR INDIVIDUALS

UNITED BROTHERHOOD OF CARPENTERS LOCAL 964
William V. Hamilton - William A. Sopko

INTERNATIONAL BROTHERHOOD OF ELECTRICAL WORKERS LOCAL 363
Cosmo Damiani

VILLAGE OF SPRING VALLEY
Joel Rosenthal, Mayor

CHAPTER 7

EXPANSION AND GROWTH, 1988-1991
10th, 11th Remembrance Day Programs
5th Educators Conference

The opening of the Center was a milestone but in no way a culmination of the goals of teaching, commemorating, and perpetuating the lessons of the Holocaust. As Harry Reiss commented on the fruition of six years of hard work as quoted by staff reporter Louis Lavelle in *The Journal News*: "It is a very nice feeling, but more important is that the Center will teach the young." The Center was to be open to the public from noon to 4 PM, Monday through Thursday. Holocaust Board members took on the responsibility in lieu of paid staff of opening the Center several Sundays per calendar year. In time, this task was supplemented by paid and unpaid volunteers, and eventually supplanted entirely by a paid staff person. The Center also printed a brochure, outlining the history of the Center and illustrating its exhibit space, with funds donated by the Rockland Section of the National Council of Jewish Women.

At the June 1988 meeting, a new slate of trustees was presented and accepted, keeping the tradition of staggered terms of office. One-year trustees included Esther Clifford, Anita Finkelstein, Morris Schwartz, Jack Schloss, Gloria Ziesel, Charlotte Lee, Mike Jacobs, Esther Ingber, and Manny Polak. Two-year trustees were Warren Berbit, Norman Bleckner, Robert Finkelstein, Georgine

113

Hyde, Ilse Loeb, Mimi Kirsch, Sam Simon, Sam Weinberger, Alaine Tamberlaine, and Rita Davis. Three-year trustees were Lillian Adler, Joseph Adler, Percy Goldstein, Anne Katz, Martin Goldstein, Joseph Warburg, Jacques Gerstenfeld, Karl Hess, and Phyllis Goldstein. Elected officers were Rubin Josephs, President; Al Kirsch, Chairman of the Board; Dorothy Steinmetz and Esther Pal, Vice-Presidents; Harry Reiss, Executive Secretary; and Monte Melamed, Treasurer.

On January 5, 1989, the first meeting of the new year after the opening of the new building, which itself was the culmination of more than eight years of work, included in its agenda, besides the usual reports from the treasurer and the different committees— building, education, fundraising, membership, newsletter, Remembrance Day, and Second Generation and Survivors, two exhortations to the Board: (1) "you MUST be a member of the Center in order to remain on the Board of Trustees"; (2) "you MUST notify the director if you plan to be absent. Our By-laws state that 3 UNEXPLAINED ABSENCES WILL RESULT IN REMOVAL FROM THE BOARD." The capitalization made the point loud and clear. Of the 34 members of the Board of Trustees and 10 members of the Honorary Board of Governors, the minutes listed only 15 in attendance: Norman Bleckner, Esther Clifford, Jacques Gerstenfeld, Karl Hess, Georgine Hyde, Esther Ingber, Rubin Josephs, Anne Katz, Charlotte Lee, Ilse Loeb, Monte Melamed, Harry Reiss, Judith Siegelbaum, Alaine Tamberlaine, and Bernie Weiner. This issue of non-attendance was to be an ongoing mantra for more than two decades of Board meetings. The three-absence threat of removal, however, has never been enforced although the size of the Board did vary from more than 30 members to its most compact size of 18 in more recent history. Attendance, involvement, and fundraising gradually predominated meeting agendas as the organization settled into its consolidation phase.

From 1988 through 1995, Board positions were essentially those of Chairman of the Board, President, Vice-Presidents, Executive-Secretary, Treasurer, and Managing Director. The terms of the managing director reflected the thrust of the organization over the course of the next two and a half decades. The position was held by Frances Sternberg (briefly in 1987), Bernard Wiener (1988-1995), and Barbara Grau (1995-2004), during which period it remained a part-time position. The latter two were both were retired teachers from the East Ramapo School system. The title of "managing director" morphed into "executive director" after Wiener's retirement, and upon Barbara Grau's appointment. Harry Reiss, who had served as unpaid Administrative Director, Executive Director, and then Executive Secretary, assumed the new Board position of Executive Vice-President in 1991; another new position, that of Recording Secretary, had been added in 1990, and filled by Barbara Scheinson. Bernard Weiner and Barbara Grau, perhaps because each had been educators, focused primarily on promoting and overseeing the school group visits to the Center, which became an almost daily occurrence. Although both were technically part-time directors, they managed to supervise the working of the Center in every aspect, down to the shoveling of snow off the front steps. The office staff consisted of one part-time secretary, and special events were run by members of the Board. Harry Reiss continued to chair the Holocaust Remembrance Day Program, with the Remembrance Day Committee, as well as participating in the Kristallnacht program, every year. The Educators Conferences were planned and carried out by a committee, consisting at various times mainly of Reiss, Barbara Grau, Bernie Wiener, and Rita Davis, and chaired by Georgine Hyde, who during this period was also president of the East Ramapo School Board.

Barbara Grau retired in 2002 and was replaced briefly by Moses Weintraub, also a retired educator, who left the position after a few months. Grau then returned, but retired officially in 2004. Over the next six years, four persons held the Executive Director position: Rabbi Michael Gisser, Rabbi Rick Harkavy, Moses Bierman, and in 2010 Tanja Sarett.

Rabbi Michael Gisser was the first to take up the directorship as a full-time position, with the expectation that the fundraising and management aspects of the Center would be professionally administered in lieu of the volunteer Board. The expanded duties of the director eventually led to the need for an educational director to oversee the school groups and the Center's educational programs. As the administrative staff grew in size, the budget also rose, and the need for fundraising became paramount in Board discussions. The Center applied for museum status in the hope that this step would create eligibility for more government grants. By the beginning of the second decade of the 21st century, the Center had reached something resembling "maintenance" stage, whereby keeping financially afloat surpassed all other considerations. The question arises whether this condition will lead to a reorganization and revaluation of its mission, perhaps taking the Center back to its original, idealistic stage.

The financial report submitted to the Board of Directors on February 16, 1989, bears an uncanny resemblance to subsequent reports in substance and proportion, if not actual numbers. A restricted account of $22,295 was allotted at that time for the Siegelbaum Lecture Series. A checking account earmarked for "operating budget" held $15,888, and a reserve account for Capital Building $10,000, making for a total balance of cash on hand of $48,183. The Center's annual budget in those years was approximately $115,000. Funds were sought from the New York State Legislature, as well as from the local UJA. For the fiscal year 1988-89, grants from New York State and local governments totaled $32,500, and a grant of $3,300 was received from the UJA. Outstanding pledges from individuals and businesses totaled $88,445.

Letters written by the Center's president Rubin Josephs to State Senator Eugene Levy and to UJA Acting Chair Mark Greenberg attested to the ongoing nature of the search for funding.

The Center's Usage Report of May 1989 stated that the facility had counted 600 visitors on Opening Day, 768 prior to opening day, 250 on Kristallnacht (for an activity held at the Center), and 1,840 drop-in visitors (1,420 of whom had signed in). In addition, student groups totaled 5,394 (2,800 from non- Jewish schools), for a grand total of 8,852 visitors. If the 700-800 attendees at the Annual Remembrance Day program were added to the figure, the Center that year played host to approximately 10,000 people. It numbered some 1,700 paid- up members.

Plans for the next Educators' Conference, scheduled for November 6, 1989, began to be formulated. It was to be held in the Finkelstein Library and would include a tour of the Museum's exhibits for the participating educators. A search would be made for an author of a "significant work" to be the keynote speaker. This turned out to be David Wyman, who had written *The Abandonment of the Jews*. More than two decades later, in 2011, Marion Reiss approached Professor Wyman at a seminar on America's role during the Holocaust years that was held at Yad Vashem in Jerusalem and at which he was the keynote speaker. She asked if he recalled Harry Reiss and the Rockland Center for Holocaust Studies. Without missing a beat, Wyman replied: "Yes, it was held in a library room wasn't it - for teachers? I remember it well." Such was the influence that the Center was already having on the

Professor D. Wyman responds to the questions of educators at the November 6 Teacher's Conference

world of Holocaust studies. The conference was jointly sponsored, thanks to Georgine Hyde, by the Board of Cooperative Educational Services of Rockland County (BOCES) and the Holocaust Center. This 5th Educator's Conference was chaired by Barbara Grau, along with conference committee members Rita Davis, Harry Reiss, and Bernard Weiner.

At this February Board meeting, Harry Reiss announced the date for the 10th Remembrance program, May 7, 1989. Esther Clifford, who represented the Survivors Committee, announced that it was still holding events that particular year in Rivervale, New Jersey. Anne Katz gave the report of the Second Generation group, which was holding elections for its own officers. Bernard Weiner announced an upcoming reception in honor of Spring Valley Mayor Joel Rosenthal. A calm had settled over the Board as it basked in the first year of its celebratory opening ceremony.

Many threads weave through the history of the Center. On February 22, 1989, Weiner wrote a letter to Mr. Michael Bierman, congratulating him on his appointment as executive director of the United Jewish Community of Rockland County and inviting him to "arrange a visit here [the Center] to see firsthand what the Center is accomplishing." Almost 20 years later, Bierman would assume the position of Executive Director of the Holocaust Museum and Study Center as it later was called. Wiener, who by that time had long since retired from Center activity, had recently passed away.

In April 1989, the Center observed a moment of silence at its Board Meeting in memory of Monte Melamed, who had served as its Treasurer. Trees were to be planted in his memory, and a plaque put up in the Center. The Center was offered two videotapes: one depicting a recent visit to Germany by Walter and Ilse Loeb; and the second, a copy of a video created by Rockland Community College of the Center's exhibition for use in the College's Holocaust Studies program.

In a letter to the members of the Board and to Sam Simon, Directory of the Finkelstein Library, dated May 3, Al Kirsch, Chairman of the Center Board, broached the topic of a name change that would incorporate the word "Museum." He proposed: "Rockland Center and Museum for Holocaust Studies." It would take almost a decade for a name change to go into effect, the Holocaust Center for Holocaust Studies being renamed the "Holocaust Museum and Study Center" in October 2001.

Financial support came in various forms, some planned and some not. Thus, it received a surprise donation of almost $5,000 from the trustees of the Rockland County Day School upon that institution's closing early in 1989. Another example: a business luncheon sponsored by Orange and Rockland Utilities president Thomas Griffin Jr. and former Rockland County Treasurer Joseph St. Lawrence brought in more than $25,000.

The 10th annual Remembrance Day Program was held, as usual at Ramapo Senior High School, on May 7, 1989. The topic, "Europe on the Eve of Destruction," featured the recollections of five Rockland County residents who had lived in Europe at the start of Hitler's reign of terror. Joseph Adler, Irene Goudsmith, Edith Kling, Esther Clifford, and Ilse Loeb each recalled the dread they felt as Jews became isolated and demonized in Germany

Courtesy of The Journal News

and Austria during the 1930's. Clifford described life in Germany after Hitler had gained power as "utter despair. I will never forget; I never have; and I never will." Adler, who escaped from Czechoslovakia, expressed his gratitude for the freedom he enjoyed in the United States. Harry Reiss summed up the deprivation of liberties in the 1930's: "Freedom is a very fragile commodity."

The spring of 1989 also saw a series of lectures by Rockland County Rabbis, including Rabbi Pernick of Beth Am Temple in Pearl River, Rabbi Ron Mass of Temple Beth El in Spring Valley, and Rabbi Robert Hirt of Yeshiva University, who resided in Monsey.

At the nominating committee meeting in the Spring of 1989, a question that had been previously discussed reemerged: Should the Center's Board include non-Jewish members? Emotions on both sides of the issue were very strong, ranging from the feeling that Center policy should not be made by the general public to the opinion that the Center should be concerned with the larger issues of humanity. It was decided to put aside the issue for the present time. As it happened, the question was kept in the drawer for five years, taken out once again at a Board meeting on February 17, 1994, at which time it was pointed out that this was really a non-issue: the Center's By-Laws specifically stated that the Board was non-discriminatory. In subsequent years, several non-Jewish board members sat on almost every Board. The slate for the new Board in 1989 reflected the 1, 2, and 3-year step-down terms: 1- year trustees were Norman Bleckner, Anita Finkelstein, Ed Krupnik, Ellen Kronethal, Manny Polak, Frances Melamed, Dorothy Steinmetz, Alaine Tamberlaine, and Gloria Zeisel; two-year trustees were Morris Schwartz, Rita

Davis, Robert Finkelstein, Georgine Hyde, Mimi Kirsch, Sam Simon, Lillian Adler, Jacques Gerstenfeld, Martin Goldstein, and Joseph Weinberg; three-year trustees were Esther Clifford, Charlotte Lee, Mike Jacobs, Warren Berbit, Ilse Loeb, Samuel Weinberger, Karl Hess, and Joseph Adler. Officers were President, Al Kirsch; Chairman of the Board, Ruby Josephs; Vice Presidents, Judy Siegelbaum, Esther Schulman, and Anne Katz; Executive Secretary, Harry Reiss; and Treasurer, Alan Koss.

On June 20, 1989, the Center held an Awards Presentation program, at which a special Acts of Courage award was presented to Art and Johanna Vos, who had been responsible for saving Ilse Loeb during the war. Awards were also presented to three students who had won the essay and creative writing contest sponsored by the Center.

The 5th Educator's Conference was planned, as mentioned for November 6, 1989, with David Wyman as the event's main speaker. An interesting story reveals how the Center obtained a second speaker for this event, Annette Dumbach, author of *Shattering the German Night – Story of the White Rose*. Several months before the conference, Estelle Barasek, who worked with Marion Reiss at LaGuardia High School of the Arts in Manhattan and who had attended a previous conference at the Center, mentioned the name of a friend who had written a book about the Holocaust. The friend, Annette Dumbach, who had grown up in the Bronx, had been a

Annette Dumbach, co-author of "Shattering The German Night: The Story of The White Rose", conducts a workshop at the November 6 Teachers Conference, held at the Finklestein Library. The workshop focused on the use of literature in teaching the Holocaust.

Fulbright Scholar in Germany, where she remained and married a German engineer. Her original research into the White Rose organization, a group of university students who had been one of the few groups to oppose Adolph Hitler, distributing anti-Nazi party flyers and stirring up student opposition to Nazi policies, until its members were finally caught and murdered, was translated into many languages and became a very popular book in Europe.

This was before the days of prolific email, and the question arose as to how Ms. Dumbach could be contacted and asked to participate in the conference. Estelle called Annette's sister for the address and learned that the Dumbachs were now living in Egypt, where Annette's husband was working on an engineering project for the German government. Marion Reiss began to laugh at this seemingly regrettable report, however, because she and Harry were planning a four-day El Al special trip from Israel to Egypt that very Spring. Would it be possible for them to meet in Cairo? Estelle happily reported that Annette would be delighted to meet the Reisses. Annette and her husband met Harry and Marion at their hotel the very first night and, as they drank Coca Cola together, finalized plans for the Educators' Conference within the hour.

In the summer of 1989, Harry Reiss attended a month-long seminar at Yad Vashem, where 25 participants from all over the world studied with scholars and authors who were involved in Holocaust teaching or research. It was a seminal experience for Harry, and he rekindled acquaintanceships, including that of Sister Rose Thering of Seton Hall University, who was also a participant in the Seminar. Marion, who at the same time was doing volunteer teaching at the Amalya School, where she and Harry lived for a month, located not too far from Yad Vashem, also participated in some of the talks and trips. One of the tours was to Nes Amin, a kibbutz in the western Galilee established by Christians after the war to show solidarity with

Israel and the Jewish people. At one point in the visit, though, the seminar participants were ushered into an auditorium, where they were given a speech that sounded very much, as Reiss put it, "like a missionary pitch." After it was over, Marion turned to Sister Rose Thering, who was seated right behind them, and asked what she thought of the talk. The Catholic educator smiled broadly and said: "Marion, this was an example of a charismatic presentation, meaning a missionary presentation." During this seminar, new photos of the children of the Lodz Ghetto were privately displayed to the participants. Harry was particularly taken with pictures of the children's drawings of their lives in the textile workshops. He requested copies of the photos from Yad Vashem, which were sent to him on his return to New York. To emphasize how protected these slides were at that time, Shulamit Imbar, of Yad Vashem, wrote to Harry: "We no longer sell the above slides. Nevertheless, we are sending them to you honoring our prior commitment. We would very much appreciate therefore you're not advertising these slides in any way, because they are no longer for sale, although, of course, you can use them in your lectures." On March 13, 1991, Harry presented them at the Center during a lecture he delivered, called "Needles and Thread." This was the first time the photos had been exhibited in the United States.   Many years later, in 2009, while participating in a seminar on Holocaust Education at Yad Vashem, Marion tracked down the story behind the slides from Shulamit Imbar, who was then serving as Education Director at Yad Vashem. The slides are now available to teachers in book form in both English and Hebrew.

Toward the end of 1989, a new idea for a fundraiser emerged – a biannual Journal Dinner, as opposed to an occasional event, which would both bring publicity to the Center through its honorees and also raise much-needed funds. A tentative date, September 9, 1990, was publicized for the event. It was hoped that the price of the dinner could be kept down to $75 so as to attract the largest possible turnout. An unexpected result of the announcement of the event was a letter to Harry from the Hudson Valley Political Action Committee, which protested the choice of date. Although HUVPAC, as it was called, had not yet selected a date for its own dinner, it wanted to have the choice of dates in September and without another county-wide Jewish organization holding its event in such proximity to theirs. Feelings ran high as they tended to do in these matters. The matter was finally resolved after a meeting between Dr. Mendy Ganchrow, President of HUVPAC, and a Center committee, consisting of Al Kirsch, Karl Hess, and Joe and Lillian Adler, led to an agreement in which the HUVPAC group would have its dinner in mid-October.

The Center Journal-Dinner which took place in September had as its honorees, Robert Finkelstein and Kenneth Gribetz and was a successful fundraiser, earning $50,000 or the Center.

By the end of 1989, Center membership amounted to more than 2,000. Plans were going ahead for the 11th Remembrance Day program, as well as for a joint program with Bergen Community College.   At the December meeting, the Center voted, on the recommendation of its Treasurer, Alan Koss, to set up an Endowment Fund, which could be used to borrow against in order to provide financial cover for future events.

The year's end also saw the culmination of negotiations for the rental of the Center from the Finkelstein Library; very helpful in this regard were Warren Berbit, Assemblyman Sam Colman, and State Senator Eugene Levy, the latter two receiving letters of appreciation. In a letter to Berbit, the Center's President Al Kirsch expressed the gratitude of the Board for his legal efforts in "bringing the issue to solution in such a sensible and professional manner." The lease for the Center was signed in April 1990; the rental fee: $1 per year. The assets of the Center that year were summarized as follows; $27,725 – cash; $24,517 – Siegelbaum Lecture Fund; $10,580 – for the Endowment Fund, with an additional $10,000 to be added overall. There were no outstanding bills. The Center counted 2,200 members and had set itself a goal of 3,000.

With the Educators' Conference just completed, a Cocktail party honoring Bill Sopko was planned for the Spring, and the Journal Dinner for the Fall—the Center was buzzing with activity. Norman Bleckner was engaged to mount an artifacts display, for which Harry was writing a grant. A year after the opening of the building, the Center was becoming a major force among Jewish organizations in Rockland County.

The 11th Annual Remembrance Day program took place, as usual, in the auditorium of the Ramapo Senior High School on April 22, 1990, promptly at 2 PM. The keynote speaker was Ruth Gruber, whose journalistic and humanitarian career had spanned decades. Her topic was "The New Anti-Semitism," which made reference to recent headlines regarding skinhead activities. She wowed the audience with her story of how she saved many European Jews, who spent the war years in Oswego, New York. April 22nd was Earth Day that year, a fact alluded to in the invocation by Rabbi Mordechai Tendler. Harry Reiss introduced the program by referring to a different kind of earth day in the not-distant past: "This is Earth Day – to extol and enjoy our

Ruth Gruber addressing audience

planet earth. At Babi Yar in Kiev in the Soviet Union in 1941, a very different scene took place on the earth, where, over several months, an estimated 100,000 Jews were stripped naked, forced to stand at the edge of large pits, and then shot, with their bodies falling into the ravine." He pointedly asked: "How could such events have taken place? Students who were born in the 1970's [and] to whom the Vietnam War is ancient history want to learn more about what happened in Europe that could have resulted in this senseless death of six million innocent men, women, and children." Perhaps with this age group in mind, the candle-lighting ceremony called up not only the second generation but their children, the third generation, as well, to light candles, once again, in memoriam.

At the next Board meeting, on May 17, 1990, the members of the Board applauded Harry Reiss and his committee for the moving program. The members of the Remembrance Day Committee at this time were Michael Bierman, Barbara Grau, Georgine Hyde, Michael Jacobs, Janice Kalish, Saul Kalish, Anne Katz, Ed Krupnick, Ilse Loeb, Marion Reiss, Judy Siegelbaum, and Judge Bernard Stanger.

The Board at this time comprised 25 members plus 8 officers; 3 new members were nominated, as well. At this meeting, the Board adopted a proposed "Artifacts/Memorabilia Policy" as follows:

1-The Center will accept items which relate to the period of Nazi ascendance, primarily 1933-1945, and the ensuing events which followed from the Nazi regime (i.e., D.P. Camps, war crimes trials, search for Nazi war criminals, etc.), except as noted below.

a-No Nazi military paraphernalia, such as uniforms, Swastika flags, weapons, dog tags, and other related items.

2-Judaica items which are offered to the Center will be evaluated by the Artifacts /Memorabilia Committee as to how they relate to the events of the Holocaust era.

3- All items which are loaned to the Center will be accepted for a period of up to one year.

4-All items donated to the Center are not given a value price but rather a disclaimer.

At the June 1990 Board meeting, only 22 of the 33 members were in attendance, and that number included a new member, Fred Pfeffer, whose name had been added after the last meeting. The next meeting, in October, unfortunately saw participation dwindle to just 10 members. By February 1991, despite the large Board membership, a call had to go out: "An effort needs to be made to get new active people on our Board!"

The question of recognizing large donations by putting up plaques resurfaced at the June 1990 meeting. An offer had been made by the Irving Laurie Foundation to donate $200,000 to the Endowment Fund. Unlike decisions made in years past, the Board voted to acknowledge such a donation with a plaque affixed to the entrance of the Museum, and to a luncheon inviting all local and state political figures.

The Center's early concept of separating its exhibits from monetary contributions now began to fade, to the point that at a Board meeting less than a year later, in April 1991, Esther Shulman pragmatically suggested that Board members should actively contact people to upgrade their donations in return for a plaque.

One of the parallel Holocaust research organizations during these years was the Annual Scholars Conference on the Holocaust and the Churches. Started by Franklin Littell and Hubert Locke in

Philadelphia in 1970 and later directed by Marcia Littell, this conference represented the cutting edge of Holocaust scholarship for several decades. The Reisses attended this conclave on their own from the very beginning, and there Harry Reiss was able to network and meet many of the people who subsequently came to support the Rockland Center for Holocaust Studies, one of whom was Rabbi Irving Greenberg. In 1989, Harry was invited to present a paper on the topic of "Development of Holocaust Education, County, State, Nation" at the 1990 conference, which was to be held at Vanderbilt University. Later on, others in the Center requested that the Board finance their attendance at this and other events. Harry, however, was adamant about not receiving any recompense for anything that he did connected with the Holocaust Center or, indeed, Holocaust studies. He continued to attend the conferences, along with his wife, at his own expense even when he was presenting a paper. (The only exception to this principle was the course he taught on the History of the Holocaust, which was part of his assigned program at Rockland Community College.)

CHAPTER 8

CONSOLIDATION AND CONFLICT, 1991-1995
Sixth and Seventh Educators Conferences
12th, 13th, 14th, and 15th Remembrance Day programs
The Children's Wall Exhibit

Through the 1980's and 1990's, Harry Reiss as Executive Secretary undertook the writing of grants to secure money for the Center. These efforts were largely successful. In 1985, for example, a grant had been obtained from the New York State Education Department for $40,000, designated for the construction of the interior of the Center. Another from New York State, in May 1988, signed by Helen Volk of the Commission on Education, in the amount of $5,000 was designated for "workshops, conferences and lectures for educators and the general public on the social and ethical implications of the Holocaust." In 1989, the Center received $10,000 further from the State. In 1990, the Natural Heritage Trust of New York State awarded it $10,000 after several years of the Center's submitting documentation in regard to the setting up of an artifacts display in the museum part of the Center. Often, it took months of application forms and vouchers before the Center actually received the grant money. Thus, a grant for $2500 obtained from Assemblyman Alex Gromack's office in Albany in the Fall 1994 for the purchase of a copying machine required several hundred pages of documentation.

One of the most laborious of these efforts related to the request for a grant from the Natural Heritage Trust of the State of New York, for a Children's Wall and Study Center. As early as January 21, 1991, Harry Reiss wrote to Assemblyman Colman: "As per our discussion concerning proposed special legislative grant of $10,000 for . . . a proposed Children's Wall and Study Center that we plan to construct over the next few years in stages depending on grants and donations. The exhibition will convey to school-aged children the potential danger to individual rights, life, and liberty in allowing hatred of any particular race, religion, or ethnic group to grow within a country." The grant obtained for the Center by Assemblyman Colman was finally received in January 1993, along with the stipulation that a full outline of products was to be disclosed to the grantor. Correspondence regarding the grant that had begun with the Fund's administrators continued in September 1994 and lasted into 1995 in regard to the completion of the full proposal. The original concept of the Children's Wall had been proposed by Norman Bleckner, who envisioned a wall of children's faces. This was to be accompanied by a children's study center, with audio-visual equipment and materials suitable for different age groups. Reiss was appointed chairman of a committee to draw up plans for the creation of the new facility. This seemingly simple task, however, was to become a source of contention over the next few years.

The year 1991 saw solid achievements for the Holocaust Center: the 6th Educators' Conference, this one on "Ethical Implications for the 21st Century," took place at Rockland Community College. One of the panels, moderated by

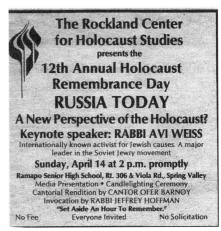

Reiss, dealt with the Spanish and Italian Holocaust. April 14, 1991, was the date set for the 12th Annual Remembrance Day Program, dedicated to "Russia Today: A New Perspective on the Holocaust." The keynote speaker was Rabbi Avi Weiss, who not only was in the forefront of the fight for the rights of Jews in the Soviet Union, but who also had recently fought against the building of a convent at Auschwitz. Rabbi Weiss addressed the issue directly in his talk: "The placement of the convent is not inadvertent," he said, but a "concealed attempt to revise history. About 10% of those killed at Auschwitz were Christians, but they were killed for their political beliefs, not their religion or race." Although Rabbi Weiss was a much sought- after public speaker, Harry used his influence to convince him to donate his time for the Remembrance program. The event also marked the first time that Cantor David Rosenzweig did not give the cantorial rendition; his replacement that year was Cantor Ofer Barnoy from the Monsey Jewish Center. Between 700 and 800 people attended the program.

Another event that month took place on April 21, 1991; a cocktail party honoring John Grant, Rockland County Executive, the evening was designed to raise funds for the Center. Held at the Center, the event was chaired by Anne Katz, with District Attorney Kenneth Gribetz serving as Honorary Chair. The Honorary Committee was headed by Sam Colman. In the invitation that was sent out, the arrangement of Board names foreshadowed the Center's future course. Anne Katz, who would become the Center's next president, was listed as Executive Vice-President, which office later became the conduit to the presidency. Esther Shulman was listed as Vice-President, Harry Reiss as Executive Secretary, and Barbara Scheinson as Recording Secretary. To the right of this list were positioned the names of the Treasurer, Alan Koss, and the Managing Director, Bernard Weiner.

On April 25, 1991, a personal letter was sent to Harry Reiss from then-President Al Kirsch. It read as follows: "I have appointed you to serve on the nominating committee. Please remember that the officers and board we choose for next year will be critical. We are also selecting new officers. The meeting will take place at the Center, Thursday, May 9, at 8:00 P.M. sharp. Please plan on attending." At the meeting, Harry was appointed Executive-Vice-President. Although this title theoretically put him next in line for the presidency, it essentially stripped him of the unique position he had held since the Center's inception, that of executive director or executive secretary. Although the word "executive" continued in his title, the fact of the matter was that his position of director was now to be phased out in favor of a paid director. Nonetheless, Reiss continued to be a member of almost every committee, writing grants, organizing fund-raisers, lecturing at the Educators' Conferences and other special events, chairing the Journal Committee, and of course chairing the Annual Remembrance Day Committee.

At the May meeting, Anne Katz's name was placed in nomination to be the next president of the Center, and the slate of officers was accepted.

The Center was at this time expanding its involvement in other community events, one of which was the "March of the Living." The Board decided to sponsor a high-school student with a partial scholarship, a repeated sponsorship that continued for several years. This step was partially modeled after the Dallas Holocaust Center's policy in that regard.

The total 1991 budget amounted to $109,940, with $57,165 allotted to salaries, $21,000 to administrative costs, utilities, and housekeeping, $17,955 to exhibits, $6,230 to insurance, and $6,800 to other fees. The budget for the Remembrance Day program totaled $1,300 and remained in that category throughout the years that Harry

Reiss ran the program. A membership drive, with mailings and a phonation, was planned. In October, the Board sadly marked the passing of Joe Adler, past president and one of the builders who had created the Center building The Board discussed establishing a scholarship fund in his memory.

Anne Katz, who assumed the presidency in July, reiterated in her opening remarks her emphasis on a committee system, in which each member of the Board would undertake a particular responsibility. At first, there were eight committees: Fund-raising, Arts and Artifacts, House, Membership, Community Relations, Grants, Newsletter, and Yom HaShoah. This was the first time the Remembrance Day Committee had been listed as an equal committee, rather than a separate entity.

A topic that was to recur came up at the July meeting in the form of a letter written by a resident of Monsey who objected to a photo in the museum display at the Center that included a nude woman in the death camps. Ruby Joseph argued for the importance of keeping the exhibit to underscore the horrors of that period. It was agreed to send a reply to that effect to the letter-writer. Bernard Wiener, in his capacity as Managing Director, wrote in a letter dated December 24, 1991: "Your thoughtful accolades [are] greatly appreciated. I am sorry, however, that your visit was marred by the pain you felt by the Center's singular example of frontal nudity. The committee considered the display because we felt that it was of the highest order of purpose to not only show the depths of Nazi inhumanity but to impress it upon young minds to reinforce that it must never be forgotten. That is why after much consultation and discussion, we voted to include it [and] for this reason." The question had risen before when, at the Yom HaShoah program on the Warsaw Ghetto, unretouched film footage was shown that included similar images. The line between authenticity and the sensitivity of the

Courtesy of The Journal News

Holocaust survivor and President of East Ramapo School Board Georgine Hyde and State Assemblyman Samuel Colman, D-New City, who hid from the Nazis in Poland, view an exhibit at the center

viewers was one that would repeatedly be brought up at the Center, as well as at other Holocaust centers.

In August, three new members were welcomed to the Board: Cynthia Becher, Dr. Seymour Lutwak, and Belle Rosenbaum. In a gesture covered by *Journal News* reporter Steve Lieberman, Judge and Mrs. William Zeck presented to the Center eleven volumes of the Nuremberg Trials, at which the Judge had been one of the lawyers.

As an outcome of an International Hidden Children's conference that had been held not long before this meeting, Ilse Loeb reported that she had hosted a meeting in her home of about 50 of these "hidden children" who were now living in Rockland County. Many of them, she explained, had never told their stories before. The new group, which she in essence founded, eventually put together an exhibit called "Hidden Children," which became one of the key features of the Center. The exhibit was mounted on portable boards and lent out to other museums and institutions throughout the United States. Many years later, an attempt was made to transfer them to more easily portable boards; however, the firm charged with this project unfortunately placed the photos too far down on the boards, toward the floor, making them almost visually inaccessible. The original boards were somehow compromised during the transfer; although the exhibit was remounted in the Center, it never again was loaned out.

Harry and Marion Reiss attended the International Conference on Hidden Children that was held in Jerusalem in July 1993. Entrance to the sessions was severely limited because of the emotional nature of the gathering. Harry alone, though, was allowed into the sessions because of his position at the Center. Marion was to recall how, sitting outside and listening to the conversations of participants who came outside for short breaks, she was overwhelmed with the raw emotions of grief and deprivation expressed by these "hidden children," who had survived largely from having been handed over to non-Jewish families for safe keeping. Their feelings of abandonment by their own families, even though that was what had saved their lives, were still filled with pain after 50 years. Reporting at the August Board meeting about the conference, Harry noted that "many [of the hidden children] felt they had been abandoned by their parents and had had a hard time re-adjusting after seeing their parents again."

Early in 1992, the Center received several grants, notably from the New York State Assembly, owing to the efforts of Assemblyman Sam Colman ($10,000); the Rockland County Executive Office ($4500); and Con Edison ($500). Donations to the Joseph Adler Memorial Fund, which had been set up in memory of the Center's late president, were also coming in. The Board considered putting up plaques for those who contributed more than $1,000 to this fund. Nonetheless, expenses were outstripping revenue, so that Rubin Joseph suggested at the June meeting that the Board borrow $15,000 from the interest of the Endowment Fund to cover operating expenses. This was done. The Center was considered

135

solvent, however. In a report from the accountants in June 1992, the assets of the Center were listed at $143,449. The accountants suggested moving some of the money to a second financial institution, since federally insured banking accounts at that time were limited to $100,000.

The Center periodically sponsored art shows pertaining to the Holocaust. In 1991, the artworks of Luba Krugman Gurdus were displayed. An exhibition of the artwork of Jerzy Bitter, a child survivor of the Lodz Ghetto, was displayed at the Center from January through April 1992.

Sunday, April 26, 1992, marked the 13th Annual Holocaust Remembrance Day program conducted by the Center in Rockland County. The format was the same as in previous years, with the salute to the colors by the West Point Military Color Guard, an invocation, and the traditional candle-lighting ceremony, this last joined once again by the Third Generation. The keynote speaker was Dr. Mitchell Serels of Yeshiva University, who spoke about "The Unknown Holocaust—The Sephardic Experience, 1492-1942." *The Rockland Journal News* informed readers that Europe's quarter of a million Sephardic Jews had all been targeted for extermination. In Greece, 90% of the Sephardic Jews there had been murdered. Some 700 people were reported to have attended the program, which including screening of a film, "The Hangman."

The Journal Dinner for 1992 was scheduled for November and would honor Al and Mimi Kirsch. The ads collected for these events proved a good source of revenue for the Center. Ruby Joseph suggested the addition of State Senator Linda Winikow to the Center's honoree list. Winikow had been a County legislator and was a long-time friend of the Center. Like previous events, the dinner was to be held at Singer's Hotel in Spring Valley. The Dinner Committee was very pleased when Senator Winikow called to reserve a full table for her staff, whom she joined after her address.

Reiss, Winikow, and unidentified guest

The 14th Remembrance Day program took place on April 18, 1993. The topic was "The Warsaw Ghetto," and the speaker was Prof. David Kranzler, author of To Save a World. Unfortunately, Kranzler was ill during the presentation, but he managed to deliver his talk uninterrupted. Cantor David Rosenzweig rendered his traditional and other solo selections. In the candle-lighting ceremony that concluded the program, Ilse Loeb joined Georgine Hyde.

During his performance, Cantor Rosenzweig unexpectedly introduced the performance of a female student. This generated some controversy on the issue of "kol isha" (a woman singing before men, generally forbidden by Orthodox Jews). In a subsequent written letter to the Board, Rosenzweig expressed regret in "taking it upon myself in surprising you at the Holocaust gathering by introducing one of my young choir students to participate along with me. Since this was not a synagogual function, I certainly felt that this young girl was not out of place. . . . Perhaps you would like to enlighten and refresh some memories with the following information of those great cantors of yesteryear that sang in orthodox synagogues with female voices." The ultra-sensitive issue of "kol isha" would resurface again and again in many different venues.

In still another event that took place that year, Harry Reiss teamed with Dr. David Beisel of Rockland Community College to present a special Holocaust Remembrance program at the college.

The topic was "The Warsaw Ghetto," and the participants consisted of a panel of students, with Reiss and Beisel moderating the discussion. The College would continue to hold annual Holocaust Remembrance Day events under Harry's leadership for many years.

On April 22, 1993, the Rockland Holocaust Center was represented by Harry and Marion Reiss and Walter and Ilse Loeb at the opening of the United States Holocaust Museum in Washington, D. C. Harry's feelings at this event were reported in an article in *The Journal News* on May 5, 1993:

"The sky was a dull granite gray with a chill, whipping rain falling, and it matched the color of the industrial looking building with its echo of European factory windows and towers. All of it was new but familiar and sinister at the same time. The ground was wet, muddy clay made deeper and more clinging by the steady milling of the crowd of more than 4,000 men, women, and children in the clearing in front of the platform. The plastic chairs were wet and clothing and shoes were getting soaked right through rain gear and galoshes…Some of the people had been there for almost three hours waiting for the ceremony to begin…People were getting agitated: children were crying, older people were sniffling and coughing."

The Reisses at the US Holocaust Museum

"Outside the immediate area, neo-Nazi groups were shouting, 'Move it to Europe. Don't listen to the lies of the Jews. The Holocaust is a lie—it never happened.' Was this the way it was 50 years ago—all over Europe, when an Aktion was starting to take place? One of the people said: 'The S.S. made us stand in this kind of weather for 8 to 10 hours at a time while they counted us off.' Walter Loeb described his incarceration in Dachau after Kristallnacht; his wife Ilse remembered the Dutch family who risked their lives hiding her and other Jewish refugee children.

"Then, the sun came out and it wasn't Poland in 1943 but Washington D.C. on April 22, 1993. As my wife Marion said: "We weren't waiting to be taken to the trains for resettlement – thousands of survivors and their children were waiting for the President to dedicate the U.S. Holocaust Museum." The military band was a U.S. Army Band – the Army that liberated Nazi camps in 1945. The youthful couple walking onto the platform was our new President [Bill Clinton] and his wife. Was I crying when the chorus of students from the Alice Deal Junior High School began to sing an Eastern-Europe/ Yiddish folk song? Why did I feel both joy and sadness when the President said, referring to the hate group outside the area: 'They are free to say what they want to, but they are the reason why we must have this museum in our nation's capital.' Did I just imagine that everyone at the dedication was so moved by the stirring words of 'America the Beautiful' – and 'bless thy good with brotherhood from sea to shining sea'?"

In June 1993, the Art and Artifacts Committee, newly chaired by Belle Rosenbaum and Gloria Zeisel, reported that after discussions with Judith Peck, an art professor at Ramapo College in New Jersey, and member of ACOR (Arts Council of Rockland), and following a press release that had called for artistic renditions, a winning concept for the Children's Wall, created by the artist Ed Cohen, had been chosen. There would be a hanging rectangular wall featuring over 1,000 Stars of David cut out, with light showing from behind. The plan was to sell each star for $100 in memory of a child who had perished in the Holocaust. Adjacent to the wall would be an inscription of past president Joe Adler's name. This entire design was later argued over and continually modified until the final plan was completed. The completed wall itself cost $7800. A separate but related Children's Wing that had been discussed never, however, materialized. At this meeting, a new member of the Board, Norman Garfield, a WRKL radio announcer and journalist who thereafter volunteered to become a member of the Arts and Artifacts Committee, spoke very emotionally about the Children's Wall. His passionate involvement eventually led to a tense situation as will be described later.

By the August meeting, the Arts and Artifacts committee was complaining that it had not yet received money to start construction of the wall; furthermore, it did not know what to do with the other art works that had been submitted, as well as with a Torah scroll that had been donated previously. The issue of the artistic rendering for the wall was still outstanding in December, when artist Ed Cohen was invited to meet the Board. It requested that he provide a final rendering of the project, which was submitted in February 1994 and accepted.

That summer, Belle Rosenbaum loaned to the Center for an indefinite period of time a bronze sculpture by Julia Balk entitled "Waiting", and the agreement for its acceptance would become the prototype for future acquisitions. Essentially, it laid the groundwork for the continuous display of the sculpture, with the donor's name prominently affixed to the work. It was to remain donated to the Center as long as the latter kept it on display on the premises. The Center was also required to maintain the sculpture and to insure it in the amount of $10,000.

A program on the Danish rescue of the Jews was planned for the Fall. Rabbi Nathan Bamberger of the Kingsbridge Heights Jewish Center in the Bronx, who was a survivor of that rescue effort, was invited to be the guest speaker, along with Leif Donde, the New York Consul of Denmark.

Several fundraising activities were planned, among them a tour for Board members of the U.S. Holocaust Museum in Washington and, in the spring, a Cocktail Reception, featuring Christopher Browning , author of *Ordinary Men*. Sister Rose Thering, who had spoken at the inaugural reception, was invited back to give a lecture on May 10, 1994, which was very well attended and received. The event was attended by community leaders, Dominican nuns and Center members.

At this time, a new secretary was appointed, Barbara Posner, who would stay with the Board until 2004, when Barbara Grau retired.

In March 1994, Harry Reiss traveled to Berlin to present a paper at a conference at Humboldt University aptly titled, "Remembering for the Future" and designed to deal with some of the issues of recurring anti-Semitism in Germany. The program included many distinguished Holocaust scholars, including Professor Yehuda Bauer, Dr. Frank Littell, and Dr. Michael Berembaum. Reiss captioned his paper, "Academic and Community Involvement in Teaching the Ethical and Cultural Values of the Holocaust and Its Aftermath." He later wrote about his experiences at this international conference that had taken place on German soil. Harry's "Impressions of Berlin," published in *The Jewish Herald* in its March 1995 issue, juxtaposed two experiences that seemed to contradict each other.

He wrote:

"On the eve of Passover 1994 in Luebeck, a small group of German Jews planned to have their first Passover Seder in a synagogue destroyed in 1938 and rebuilt in the 1960's. Neo-Nazis fire-bombed the room in the synagogue that was to be used. In other towns there were desecrations of cemeteries, Jewish memorials, and attacks on foreigners. The following night, a protest rally against these incidents was held by 5000 Berliners. On the plane back to the United States, a steward served 'Herr Reiss' a completely enclosed 100% kashar (Kosher) dinner with the words: *You are*

Reiss in Berlin

the only one on the plane receiving this special meal. And I wondered – What are we "Remembering for the Future"?

Several weeks later, precisely at 2 PM on Sunday, April 10, 1994, the 15th Annual Remembrance Day Program commenced at Ramapo Senior High School. Harry Reiss referred to his recent trip to Germany in his opening remarks. He commented: "A question was recently raised by a Jewish publication: 'Are American Jews obsessed with the Holocaust? Do we have to dwell on the troubles?' I certainly cannot answer that question, but having just returned from a conference in Berlin on the renewed anti-Semitism in Germany, I can tell you that in Berlin whenever I was given instructions for finding the few— very few— institutions of Jewish communal life left in Berlin, I was always told, 'Don't worry, you won't have any trouble finding it – you will see the police outside.' I can tell you to paraphrase the famous phrase 'Eternal Vigilance is the price of liberty.' Here in America we know that liberty is granted only to those who love it, and are always ready to guard and defend it."

The keynote speaker on that Remembrance Day, Dr. Yaffa Eliach, addressed the topic, "Miracle of the Hidden Children." A professor at Brooklyn College, author of *Hassidic Tales of the Holocaust*, and creator of the "Tower of Faces" at the United States Holocaust Museum, Dr. Eliach had been hidden herself as a child after the murder of most of her fellow villagers in Egszyszki, Poland. She recalled standing many years later as a survivor at the graves of her relatives and friends  and hearing "the victim's voices begging to be remembered." Wishing to keep their memories alive as they had been in life, not as skeletons, she began gathering photos of the villagers from before the war, the faces of 800 children who were killed there. So moving was her address that as the survivors and their children came to light memorial candles, the room went silent for a full minute before Cantor Barnoy began to chant the memorial prayer. The emotions in the auditorium were as raw as they had been at the very first Remembrance program.

The year 1994 saw a number of changes in the Center that would influence its future for years to come. First, Anne Katz completed her term as President of the Center, and Harry Reiss was elected the new President. Anne Katz's farewell letter to the Board, thanking its members for "their time, spirit and especially friendship," came just a few days before Bernard Weiner's resignation letter in June. He expressed his thanks for the success of his six and one-half years as the Center's Managing Director. The incoming director,

Barbara Grau, officially began her term on July 1, 1994, with the new title, Executive-Director.

Although now elected President of the Center, with all the prestige it evoked, Harry Reiss might certainly have preferred to retain his original unpaid position as Executive Director, given to him at the establishment of the Center. However, Harry and Barbara worked well together in the ensuing years; their mutual respect and similar educational backgrounds (they had both begun their educational careers teaching history at George Washington High School in Manhattan) made an eventual "meetings of minds" almost inevitable. Later that year, Harry, who had also retired from the New York City Board of Education, decided to run for local public office. Following his election to the Ramapo Town Board in November, he invited Grau and the entire Center Board to his induction ceremony in December 1994.

The 7th Educators' Conference was to be held at Rockland Community College on Monday, December 5, 1994, with the theme, "Hate, Then and Now." Frank Littell, founder of the Conference on the Holocaust and the Churches, would be keynote speaker. Workshops were led by Dr. George Gregory of the New York State Education Department, Dr. Michael Dobkowski of Hobart and William Smith Colleges, Dr. David Beisel of Rockland Community College, Mark Weitzman of the Simon Wiesenthal Center, and Dr. Fred Letzter of Nyack Public Schools. Harry chaired the workshop led by Dr. Beisel, titled "Ordinary People: Instruments of Hate."

The 8th Educators' Conference, co-sponsored by the Holocaust Center and BOCES, would be held on November 13, 1997, at the Stony Point Conference Center in the northern part of Rockland County. The keynote speaker for the topic, "Techniques for Integrating Holocaust Studies into Tomorrow's Curriculum," was Peter Nelson, Director of the "Facing History and Ourselves"

Foundation. Presenters included Judge William Zeck, Susan Colton from East Ramapo School District, John Weiss of Hunter College, Dr. Karen Shawn of Moriah School, and Dr. Maria Rosenbloom, a survivor and Professor of Social Work at Hunter College. The conference also included a breakout session on library investigation, with the participation of Evelyn Daks, Nick Rossi, Erica Grodin, Elise Krakower and Maureen Shields, Ann Hein, and Elinor Garfinkel.

A second Board trip to Washington and the Holocaust Museum was being planned, with a hoped-for profit for the Center of more than $3,000.

By May of 1994 work on the Children's Wall had begun. The Art and Artifacts Committee asked Board members to submit short sayings for the wall and chose the color blue for the background. A new idea was to accompany the design with memorial plaques on the adjacent wall that would be sold to members. As early as April, before her retirement, Anne Katz had invited Board members to submit ideas for wording or inscriptions for the sculpture. In June, Committee co-chair Gloria Zeisel reported that she hoped the Children's Wall would be completed and installed by August.

Harry Reiss was absent at the August meeting, which was chaired by Executive Vice-President Sam Simon. At that meeting, Norman Garfield reported that he had set up a special sub-committee to work on the wording to be used on the Children's Wall and that this group, which did not include the co-chairs of the Arts and Artifacts Committee, Gloria Zeisel and Belle Rosenbaum, had unanimously chosen these words: "A Generation Lost, 1,500,000 Children." Gloria Zeisel reported that the Arts and Artifacts committee had met separately and decided on another wording: "Even the Heavens Shed Tears for the Children." Al Kirsch moved that the committee meet with the artist and combine both statements.

145

The motion was passed, with the addendum that all future committees must be appointed by the president.

Installation had already begun on the Children's Wall, when Norman Garfield reminded the Board at the September meeting of his suggestion, presented at the previous meeting, to place his sub-committee's wording at the top of the sculpture and the Arts and Artifacts Committee's wording at the bottom. It was agreed that Gloria Zeisel and Belle Rosenbaum, who were not at this meeting, would be consulted. Norman Garfield offered to write this out, and Harry Reiss was asked to contact Ed Cohen, Belle Rosenbaum, and Gloria Zeisel regarding the final wording and its placement. The question of the Children's Wall was to haunt the early months of Harry's presidency.

At the next meeting, on October 20th, Belle Rosenbaum announced that the Children's Wall would be completed in November but that the placement of the lettering was not yet finalized. Even though it had been agreed that both statements would be used, there was some disagreement as to which would be on top. Emotions ran high, and Harry asked Norman Garfield, Belle Rosenbaum, Gloria Zeisel, Al Kirsch, and Morris Schwartz to meet with the artist to discuss the placement of the two wordings. When the November meeting convened, however, Norman Garfield was absent, and the matter continued to be put off. Nevertheless, the remainder of the wall was proceeding toward completion, and plans were being made for its dedication in December.

Ed Cohen, the artist, was pressed for room for the placement of the lettering, since no size had been allocated for it. In the end, the raised letters for the phrase "Even the Heavens Shed Tears for the Children" took up so much space at the bottom that there was no room for lettering of equal size on top for the phrase, "A Generation Lost 1,500,000 Children." To solve the problem, the artist created a brass plaque on which he engraved this phrase and which would fit into the top of the sculpture as planned. In the ensuing melee of accusations and condemnations, a decision had to be made whether to accept this compromise or to return the plaque to the artist. Reiss, as it happened, cast the deciding vote in favor of the compromise, a decision that did not make everybody happy. The incident exemplifies how much tension could be generated by seemingly small issues in this otherwise noble enterprise of commemoration and memorial.

As it turned out, water damage in the winter of 1994 /1995 delayed the official opening of the wall, which finally took place on December 17, 1995. The Dedication ceremony was titled "The Children's Wall-In Memory of the 1,500,000 Children."

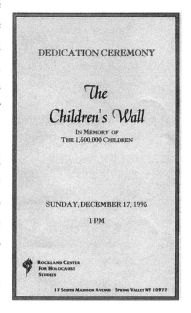

Judy Pesetzky of the Second Generation group took over the Membership chairmanship from Morris Schwartz. Reaching out to old members to renew their membership, as well as to new members, was always a priority. Phonathons were successfully used in this endeavor.

The budget for 1995 was raised to $122,150. The expense of salaries had risen from about $36,000 a few years before to $67,000. Fundraising was a paramount concern. The November 1994 meeting also responded to the loss of money incurred by the Art Show. Al Kirsch moved to have the Board give prior approval to all expenditures for Center functions in excess of $200.

The idea of asking synagogues to join as organizational members was raised by Ruby Josephs. He said that Rabbi Louis Frishman of Temple Beth-El, who was chair of the Rockland County Board of Rabbis, was agreeable to this idea.

Ilse Loeb reported that she was going ahead with her plans to set up a Hidden Children Exhibit. She brought to the Board as a new member Max Goudsmith, who had himself been a hidden child. Although she had received some support from the Rockland County Historical Society for this project, Ilse requested money from the Board, as well, to help finance it. She claimed that it could eventually raise money for the Center by becoming a traveling exhibit. The Board voted to allocate $3000 for the Hidden Children Exhibit.

A Journal – Dinner honoring Bernard Weiner on his retirement as Managing Director of the Center was planned for October 27, 1994. It would be held at the New City Jewish Center and have glatt kosher catering. It was decided to hold down the price of tickets to the dinner to $36 so that more people could afford to attend. As Weiner bade farewell to the Center, he announced that 78,000 people had made use of the Center in one way or another since its opening in 1988.

The new Board was installed in June: President –Harry Reiss; Chairman of the Board – Rubin Josephs; Executive Vice-President– Sam Simon; Vice-Presidents– Karl Hess, Susan Klein, Esther Schulman; Treasurer – Alan Koss; and Recording Secretary – Barbara Scheinson. New members inducted onto the Board were Ruchana White, Max Goudsmith, Anne Katz, and Dr. Arthur Landau. New members of the Honorary Board of Governors were Robert Finkelstein, Jacques Gerstenfeld, and Bernard Weiner.

Chapter 9

Recognitions and Recurring Themes, 1995-1998
16th, 17th, and 18th Remembrance Day Programs
Testimonial Dinner for Anne Katz and Harry Reiss

A number of Center events highlighted 1995. In February, a joint Cocktail Reception was held with the Rockland County State of Israel Bonds committee.   In recognition of Board members and friends who became "snowbirds" during the winter months, a simultaneous event was held in Florida at the home of Judy Siegelbaum and Dr Abraham Freudenheim.   Harry Reiss gave the opening remarks in Spring Valley. Referring to the 50th anniversary of the end of World War II, he asked: "The opening of the Nazi death camps exposed the Nazis' final solution for the world's view. Where are we 50 years later? The Anti-Defamation League reports an increase of anti-Semitic incidents; Holocaust deniers are calling the Holocaust a figment of Jewish-Zionist propaganda. But there are also plusses – the National Holocaust Memorial Museum in Washington, new literature and films, such as "Schindler's List," being viewed all over the United States. The Rockland Center for Holocaust Studies continues to provide the education and resources so that future generations will be alert to the dangers of ethnic, religious, and national hatred, and we continue to build the State of Israel so that it can be a beacon of light to the world."

A Reception was held at the Center on April 11 for Christopher Browning, author of the trenchant volume, *Ordinary Men*. In introducing the speaker, Harry Reiss commented on Browning's chilling observation that in spite of the massacres of 1941 in Eastern Europe, about 75% of the Jews still remained alive in 1942. But in 1943, after the "final solution" and the deportations to the death camps, in particular Belzec, Treblinka, and Sobibor, the ratio of Jews still living was exactly the reverse.

The 16th Annual Remembrance Day program took place on April 30, 1995. Titled "Fifty Years after the Holocaust," the keynote speaker was Dr. Jan Karski, a professor at Georgetown University who as a young Polish diplomat in 1943 tried to warn of the murder of the Jews of Europe. He had met with little response from the leaders of the world; when finally allowed a 10-minute audience with the President, Roosevelt told him: "First we must win the war; then we will punish the criminals." Karski expressed dismay when, in 1945, world figures professed "shock" at learning of the death camps. He commented, "They said they did not know, because it was secret; to this I say, this was a myth."

Jan Karski, who had received recognition as a Righteous among the Nations, was 90 years old when he came to Rockland County to speak at the Center's Remembrance Day program. Reiss had met Karski ten years before at a Holocaust Conference in Washington, D.C. and been impressed not only by what Karski had done and the people he had met, but by his innate modesty and humility . This latter trait was still evinced in a handwritten note to Harry, in which the aged professor outlined his travel plans, mentioning only, "P.S. cost of air ticket: $142.33 (senior citizen)." Alan Doberman, a frequent video-taper of Center events, insisted on coming to the Reiss home, where Karski was resting before the program, and could not stop taking photographs of this great gentleman. In introducing Jan Karski, Harry Reiss made reference to the recent terrorist attack in Oklahoma City. He quoted comments by stricken bystanders, who when referring to the murder of some 120 innocent people, said "How can anyone treat people this way?" and "I can understand the desire

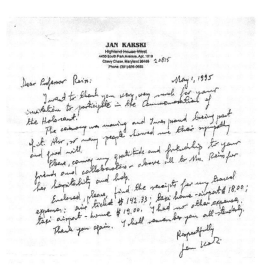

to kill adults, but why defenseless children?" Harry continued: "What can we say 50 years after the murder of not hundreds, but millions, including one and one-half million innocent children." Cantor Jacob Rosenbaum, husband of Belle Rosenbaum, delivered the cantorial renditions. The program drew an audience of 700 to 800 people.

Meanwhile, work had been going ahead on the Hidden Children Exhibit and, by April, about $7,000 had been raised. A reception, held together with the Historical Society of Rockland County, was planned for early July. In addition, a special event was planned around the Children's Wall, and plaques were being sold in denominations from $100 to $1000. A young people's art and writing competition was also being planned. In June, Barbara Grau called for the formation of a program committee so that programming would not be the brainchild of just one or two people. She indicated that she had about eight programs in mind and needed a committee to help with their realization.

On July 9, 1995, the formal opening of the Hidden Children Exhibit took place at the Historical Society of Rockland County. It had previously been agreed that after this display, the exhibit would become the property of the Center. This exhibit had been the brainchild of Ilse Loeb, who herself as mentioned had been a hidden child and years later was reunited with her rescuers. Indeed, Ilse's rescuer, Mrs. Johtje Vos, had come to Rockland to help raise funds for the exhibit. Working together with Ilse was Max Goudsmith, who had become active in the Center and would become president at a later date. The guest speaker was Professor Nehama Tec of the University of Connecticut, who had been a hidden child and had written about her experiences in Dry Tears. The exhibit, according to Harry Reiss, who had met Tec at a Conference on the Holocaust and the Churches, represented a "melding of first-hand testimony with historical expertise to produce a moving and compelling portrait of the youngest of the Holocaust survivors." This exhibit became one of the Center's most popular events and was sent out on loan to many other venues.

The sale of plaques to accompany the Children's Wall had done very well. Although most of those sold were in the $100 to $250 range, the Second Generation group was trying to raise $1000 for a group plaque.

The Center's Newsletter summed up all of these events at the end of 1995: "The Rockland Center for Holocaust Studies continues to reach out to all residents of the County and the Lower Hudson

Region. The Center has become what we hoped it to be, a beacon of truth about the Holocaust period.... Join us – the time is short but the work is great."

The topic for the April 21, 1996, Remembrance Day program dealt with the continuing attempts at Holocaust denial. Harry Reiss had been quoted previously on this subject: "All the Holocaust deniers are really about hatred. They are continuing the anti-Semitic concepts that caused the Holocaust in the first place." The keynote speaker, Dr. Lawrence Langer, a professor at Yale University and Simmons College and author of *Admitting the Holocaust* and other books, asked, "Is the Holocaust Being Trivialized?" The invocation was given by Rabbi Yisroel Saperstein, and cantorial renditions were again performed by Cantor Jacob Rosenbaum. In his presentation, Dr. Langer used a media presentation modeled on another of his books, *Holocaust Testimonies*. In answer to his question about the trivialization of the Holocaust, he said: "One way of making sure that the Holocaust is not trivialized is to pay attention to the voices of those who were there. Although we can't know what it was like, we can imagine." Unfortunately, the audio-video equipment could not do full justice to Dr. Langer's material. However, in introducing the candle-lighting ceremony, Georgine Hyde agreed with the speaker and told the audience: "Remembering is a very painful responsibility, but we cannot shirk it" Elliot Shapiro, of the Community Synagogue of Monsey, joined in on the cantorial renditions this year. Members of the committee, chaired by Harry Reiss, were Esther Clifford, Max Goudsmith, Felicia Hirschfield, Georgine Hyde, Janice and Larry Kalish Anne Katz, Ed Krupnik, Marion Reiss, Esther Schulman, Dorothy Stanger, and Anne Zuckerman. Barbara Grau also attended planning meetings. Dorothy had replaced her husband, Judge Bernard Stanger, who had passed away in November of 1995.

Hidden Children:
The Youngest Survivors of the Holocaust

Sunday, July 9, 1995
Exhibition Opening
at The Historical Society of Rockland County
20 Zukor Rd., New City, New York

The *Hidden Children: The Youngest Survivors of the Holocaust* exhibit was produced by The Historical Society of Rockland County in collaboration with The Rockland Center for Holocaust Studies and The Hidden Children of Rockland.

The Hidden Children of Rockland
Participating in the Exhibit

Leon Ginsburg

Diane Goldberg

Max Goudsmith

Simon Jeruchim

Judy Josephs

Jenny Kalsner

Cecile Kaufer

Lola Kaufman

Ilse Loeb

Irene Parkinson

Cecelia Pearlstein

Bernard Rotmil

Edith Rosen

Irene Silver

Joseph Tarko

Anne Weissman

Charlotte Wertheim

Program

Moderator – Jeffrey Keahon, President
Historical Society of Rockland County

Welcome – Harry Reiss, President
Rockland Center for Holocaust Studies
and
Ilse Loeb
The Hidden Children of Rockland

Introductions – Dr. Debra Walker, Executive Director
Historical Society of Rockland County

Remarks – Melanie Solomon, Curator
Historical Society of Rockland County

Introductions – Barbara Grau, Executive Director
Rockland Center for Holocaust Studies

**Key Note
Speaker–** Dr. Nechama Tec, Professor & Scholar
University of Connecticut

Reception to honor the Hidden Children of Rockland
following the program
at The Historical Society of Rockland County
–By Invitation Only–

154

HIDDEN CHILDREN

THE YOUNGEST SURVIVORS
OF THE HOLOCAUST

A Traveling Exhibit of
The Rockland Center for
Holocaust Studies

... "The exhibit is as powerful
as it is simple. I found myself reading
and rereading--jotting down
those words that jumped out at me
and must stay in my own memory.
I was deeply moved."

... *"A very powerful & moving exhibit."*

Nechama Tec

Later that evening, in an event of which the committee had no foreknowledge, Rabbi Saperstein who had delivered the invocation also held a Yom HaShoah Ceremony for all eleven Orthodox congregations in the county. A flyer very similar in format to the Center's had been printed up by the organizers of that event. Even students at ASHAR, a popular yeshiva day school that had previously participated in the county-wide Remembrance program, were now featured at this new event. When members of the Center complained to Harry Reiss that this might become a rival program held on the very same day, he replied: "Well, we see we have succeeded in making such commemorations more widespread. When we started, there was not even one."

At this time, the Board of Trustees numbered 39, and there were 11 members of the Board of Governors. In addition, there were Survivors, Second-Generation, and Hidden Children groups meeting at the Center.

In 1996, with Harry's term as President coming to a close, a search began for a new president. Reiss, busy with his new duties as a Town of Ramapo Councilman and with his teaching at Rockland Community College, did not want to serve a third term. Still, no one came forward to volunteer for the position. Marion Reiss suggested that Harry try to recruit Lillian Adler, whose late husband Joe had been a builder and past president of the Center. Lillian finally accepted and so began a new period in the history of the Center.

Meanwhile a testimonial Journal-Dinner was planned for Harry Reiss and Anne Katz, the two immediate past-presidents, for the fall of 1996. These dinners were very successful in raising money for the Center, bringing in at times well over $100,000. The money came mainly from Journal ads. In the Center's early years, the journal itself was a hands-on enterprise. The committee would gather the ads, proof- read them many times over, and then do the layout and page numbering. Hours and hours were spent in the MP Publishing firm in New Jersey, the committee members poring over the ads and laying out the pages across many tables that had hastily been cleared by the workers in the publishing house. The owner of the firm, Manny Polak, who became a trustee on the Center Board, gave the committee both working space and much assistance. In those years, costs were kept to a minimum by having the Journal Committee do all the legwork and proofing.

The dinner was held on November 10, 1996, but was marred for the Reiss family by the recent death of Marion's father. All of Harry's children and family members from near and far attended, however, as did most of the elected Ramapo officials and administrators with whom he had worked so closely. Marion had not planned to attend, since she was in the 30-day mourning period for her father, until Rabbi Moses Tendler told her that she had to go to the ceremonial part of the event although not the actual dinner itself, "since Harry is a public official, and people might misinterpret your absence." Georgine Hyde, one of the original three founders of the Center, insisted on presenting the award to Harry. Eleven years later, walking with a cane and assisted by a friend, she rose again to speak of Harry's achievements, but this time, sadly, at the memorial service held on the 30th day after his death, when she proclaimed: "How can I not come to eulogize Harry?"

The dinner and journal were very successful. Harry, in his remarks, looked back at the past years of the Center and, after thanking all the guests and participants, noted that his wife had hosted the Annual Remembrance Day committee meetings every year in their living room, "not to mention the early years when our home was the general mailing room for the Center." He went on to thank Assemblyman Sam Colman, who as a Rockland County legislator helped to establish the Rockland Commission, which became the

✡ **Anne Rosenberg Katz** ✡

Anne Rosenberg Katz, a past president of the Rockland Center for Holocaust Studies, founded Second Generation of Rockland County in 1983 and served as its first President from 1983-1987. Involved with the International Network of Children of Holocaust Survivors, she served as a delegate to the World Jewish Congress in Jerusalem in January, 1986. It was from this base that her involvement, care and concern with the founding and operations of the Holocaust Center began, becoming its president in 1991 and serving until 1994.

Anne's interests extend to Hadassah (Past President), Elmwood Chapter of Cancer Care, current member of the Board of Trustees of UJA/Federation of Rockland, member of the County Board of Israel Bonds and its New Leadership Committee, Trustee of Congregation Sons of Israel, Suffern.

Born in Feldafing, Germany in a Displaced Persons Camp and growing up on a chicken farm in Vineland, New Jersey, Anne went on to graduate from Long Island University with a BA Cum Laude in Sociology in 1968 and received a Masters Degree in Education from SUNY New Paltz in 1981.

Since 1976 Anne has taught kindergarten at the Reuben Gittelman Hebrew Day School and served as Administrative Assistant for the Hebrew High School of Rockland County from 1983 to 1985. Of abounding optimism, good cheer, and a capacity for hard work, Anne is deserving of all the praise we can command.

Anne and her husband Lawrence have lived in Suffern for many years with their daughter Laura and son Steven. Laura, now married, lives in Israel with her husband Jason Novich and baby daughter Talia Keren. Steven lives in Manhattan and works as a research associate in economics.

158

✡ Harry Reiss ✡

Almost twenty years ago, an article appeared in the Rockland County Journal News describing the efforts of a young adjunct professor of History at Rockland Community College to create a course on the Holocaust so that its horrors would never be repeated. That man was Harry Reiss, our Journal Dinner guest of honor, who over the next few years labored relentlessly not only to establish the Holocaust as an integral part of every history curriculum, but also to set up a Rockland Holocaust Commission modeled after the National Holocaust Commission established by the United States Congress.

The original Rockland Holocaust Commission which Harry fought to have started here in Rockland County and in which he served as Executive Secretary soon developed into the Rockland Center for Holocaust Studies where Harry continued his vital role as Executive Secretary, Executive Vice-President, and most recently, as President.

Since April of 1980, Harry has chaired the committee to honor the memory of the victims of the Holocaust in a county-wide annual Remembrance Day program at which up to 800 Rockland County citizens participate regularly.

Harry is a recently retired Supervisor with the New York City Board of Education. His efforts on behalf of troubled youngsters in School District 11 were given city-wide recognition. In addition, Harry has been an adjunct professor of History and Political Science at Rockland Community College since its inception in 1969.

Harry's interest in government and concern for community have led him to assume public office - as an elected official. Harry has been serving the people of Ramapo as Town Councilman since 1994. Prior to that he was a member of the Town of Ramapo Planning Board.

He also serves as a Board Member of the Community Synagogue of Monsey, the U.J.A. Federation of Rockland County, Mogen David Adom and ECHO.

Harry and his wife Marion, have been living in Rockland County for over thirty years. They are most proud of their children Linda and Zvi Wolicki (who live in Israel), Wendy and Yossi Shindler, Rabbi Jonathan Reiss, and grandsons Michael Shindler and Avi Wolicki.

Jonathan, Harry and Ed Reiss. Rabbi Tendler, Herb Reisman and Chris Sampson in background

Center. Harry acknowledged his co-founders, Georgine Hyde and the late Dr. Harold Siegelbaum, and went on to recall that before the 1986 Journal- Dinner, "the outside construction of the Center building was finished, seven annual Days of Remembrance programs had been held as had three successful Educators' Conferences. The Center officially opened in May 1988, [with] our initial goal of creating a permanent building for Holocaust programs, a museum, and research space for students. Today, the Rockland Center for Holocaust Studies has taken its place as an established organization in Rockland County. As a very special and unique educational and cultural organization, we need to remember and retell the lessons of the Holocaust for those who can no longer tell their experiences themselves; to commemorate the six million men, women, and children whose lives were lost in that terrible time and to educate future

The Rockland Center for Holocaust Studies

Cordially Invites You To a

Journal Dinner

in honor of

Harry Reiss
and
Anne Katz

Special Presentation to the Honorable Sam Colman

Sunday, the tenth of November
Nineteen Hundred and Ninety Six

New City Jewish Center
Old Schoolhouse Road • New City, New York

Cocktails at Six   Dinner at Seven

R.S.V.P. October 18th

Couvert $60 per person   Glatt Kosher

generations so that these events will never be repeated. When we look at the world today, there is so much sorrow that we have grown inured to terrible events. But if there is one last thought that I want to leave with you and the Center, it is that the work of the Center must make sure that no young person ever allows a violation of human rights to take place without taking strong personal action to stop it - now and in the future. May our Center continue to be a beacon of truth about the Holocaust. And may we remember that eternal vigilance is the price of liberty."

The positive feelings and sincere rapport between the two honorees, Harry Reiss and Anne Katz, were reflected in the written remarks in the Journal by the new president, Lillian Adler: "I welcome the opportunity to publicly acknowledge the dedication and hard work of our immediate two past presidents. To Anne, a child of survivors who has devoted her life to children, their education and commitment to high ethical standards, we can only say thank you and may you go from strength to strength. To Harry, an educator and administrator, whose concern and devotion to historical truth, and commitment to community shines through all he does we owe a debt of gratitude for all his years of service to the Center from its inception to the present. His inspiring efforts in ensuring our annual Day of Remembrance deserve our thanks and admirations."

Harry's college program, which had always scheduled his Holocaust course on Tuesday nights, suddenly changed to Thursday, the night of the Holocaust Center meeting. In those years, there were two meetings per month, one for the Executive Board and one for the full Board. Harry was forced to miss these meetings for several months that semester. However, he convened the Remembrance Day meetings as usual in his home, starting in November. In the meantime, Norman Garfield had been appointed by Lillian Adler to preside over a new committee to make plans for a Remembrance Day program. In a chance meeting, Marion asked Adler about this situation and informed her that plans were going ahead as usual for what would be the 18th Annual Remembrance Day program. Lillian asked whether everyone was working together. Marion assured her that everyone on the Board had been invited to participate, as had always been the case. Adler herself agreed to come to the next meeting. Faced with an uproar from past and present members of the Remembrance Day Committee, Lillian agreed to have the competing committee disbanded. She added, however, that next year, in her capacity as Center president, she would assign the Remembrance Day program to another committee.

Lillian Adler did attend and became a member of the 18th Remembrance Day Committee, which comprised, in addition to Chairman Harry Reiss, Esther Clifford, Max Goudsmith, Felicia Hirshfeld, Georgine Hyde, Janice and Larry Kalish, Anne Katz, Ed and Peggy Krupnik, Ilse Loeb, Tobe Rebhun, and Marion Reiss. The keynote speaker at the annual event was New York Congressman Charles Schumer, who spoke on the

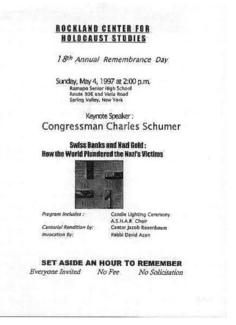

ROCKLAND CENTER FOR
HOLOCAUST STUDIES

18th Annual Remembrance Day

Sunday, May 4, 1997 at 2:00 p.m.
Ramapo Senior High School
Route 306 and Viola Road
Spring Valley, New York

Keynote Speaker:
Congressman Charles Schumer

Swiss Banks and Nazi Gold:
How the World Plundered the Nazi's Victims

Program Includes:	Candle Lighting Ceremony
	A.S.H.A.R. Choir
Cantorial Rendition by:	Cantor Jacob Rosenbaum
Invocation by:	Rabbi David Azen

SET ASIDE AN HOUR TO REMEMBER
Everyone Invited   No Fee   No Solicitation

topic of "Swiss Banks and Nazi Gold: How the World Plundered the Nazis' Victims." The ASHAR choir returned to participate in this program, as did Cantor Jacob Rosenbaum. Congressman Schumer, in reviewing the struggle for justice against the abuses of the Swiss banks, quoted Eli Wiesel: "If all the money in the Swiss banks was returned, it would not bring back the life of one Jewish child." Schumer received rousing applause when he concluded his talk with the remark: "They sought to end us. They are gone. We are here and we remember."

Harry Reiss's opening remarks at the program alluded to the fact that he had been presiding over these Remembrance Day programs since 1980, when it was the only program of its kind in the entire Hudson region. "We're proud of having been able to provide these annual programs in memory of those who perished in the Holocaust. We are most honored by your continued interest and understanding of the importance of remembering the Holocaust and passing its ethical and moral lessons to new generations so that such a tragedy will never be allowed to happen again to any group, anywhere." The members of the audience went up in file to light candles in memory of the murdered victims, but it was the last time they would do so at this annual event.

It was the end of an era for this type of program, as well. Future programs would have no calling up of survivors and their children to light a candle. Six candles alone would be lit by designated appointees.

A year later, on April 26, 1998, a photo appeared in The Rockland Journal News showing Rubin Josephs, Chairman of the Board, presenting a plaque of appreciation to Harry Reiss. The plaque

Courtesy of The Rockland Jewish Reporter

Ruby Josephs presented awards of appreciation to Marion and Harry Reiss at the Annual Rockland County Holocaust Remembrance Day program on April 26

read:

"Rockland Center for Holocaust Studies in Grateful Appreciation to Harry Reiss for Outstanding Commitment and Dedication as the Chairman of the Country Wide Commemoration Annual Day of Remembrance. 1980-1997."

The number eighteen, the number of years Harry Reiss had chaired the Remembrance Day program, represents "life" in Hebrew numerology. The Rockland County Center for Holocaust Studies, which he had been so instrumental in founding, was alive and working on the goals he had set forth so many years before. Reiss would continue to serve on the Board of Trustees and be actively involved in most Center committees and activities until his fatal stroke in 2006.

In 1998, Adler, as she had indicated, gave the program to Norman Garfield to plan. The format was changed to dual adult and children's programs. The venue was shifted to Suffern High School in the western part of Ramapo, a location that proved inconvenient for many of the residents who had attended the programs at Ramapo High School since 1980. The result was a much smaller attendance than in previous years. Suffern High School also charged a cover fee of $500. Later, the program was shifted to Rockland Community College. Garfield chaired the Remembrance Day program for the next two years, after which planning fell to a Program Committee under the direction of the Center's executive-director. In 2000, Garfield planned to hold four performances of the play "Double Crossed" for the Yom HaShoah Remembrance Day; these were to take place at Rockland Community College and at different times. The total cost of these performances amounted to $7500. The format of a single program featuring a vibrant speaker was not reinstated until years later.

Harry Reiss, meanwhile, continued to take an active role in Yom HaShoah program for Rockland Community College until 2006.

As a curious aftermath of these events, members of the Remembrance Day committee convinced Marion Reiss some time afterwards to come to a Board meeting, which she had never done before, and to protest the change in that committee. Her husband would not be in attendance, because of his college teaching commitment. Marion did attend and emotionally decried what she considered the injustice and damage to the Center of the precipitous change. At the end of her remarks, as she rose to leave, Lillian Adler and several other trustees approached her. Expecting harsh condemnation for "crashing" the meeting, she later told Harry that she was instead greeted with hugs and approbation. Shortly thereafter, she was invited to become a member of the Board herself, a position she has held till the present time.

CHAPTER 10

INSTITUTIONALIZATION AND INNOVATION, 1998 - 2005

By 1999, Marion Reiss had been elected not only to the Board of Trustees but also to the Executive Board as Secretary. Lillian Adler, who completed her term as president, was followed by Max Goudsmith, who had become involved with the Center through the Hidden Children Exhibit and been appointed to the Board in 1994. Max's son had married the daughter of Rhoda and Ed Friedman, the latter a Ramapo Town Councilman together with Harry Reiss; Rhoda had been the Chair of the Ramapo Democratic Committee. The Friedmans had always attended Holocaust functions and now, at Goudsmith's suggestion, Rhoda was appointed to the Board of Trustees. When Marion was nominated as Board Secretary, she at first demurred, citing her newness on the Board, but Rhoda Friedman convinced her to accept. Marion held this position until she resigned in early 2007 because of Harry's illness; she was reappointed in 2008 and served until 2011. In 1997, Marion completed her training as a Gallery Educator at the newly opened Museum of Jewish Heritage— A Living Memorial for the Holocaust, in New York City, and one of the first groups that she led through the new exhibits was the Board of Trustees of the Rockland Holocaust Center.

Harry had always kept his Holocaust work separate from his governmental career in order to avoid any conflict of interest. When organizations vied for grants from local governmental organizations,

Harry Reiss as President of the Center recused himself for that reason. Rhoda Friedman did not agree with this view and actively petitioned the Ramapo Town Board, which included her husband, Ed Friedman, for grants in line with those of other local governmental agencies during the time she was a trustee. Rhoda became a very active member of the Board and co-chaired, with Estelle Eisenkraft, a very successful "Buy a Brick "project, in which bricks both inside and outside the Center were dedicated "in honor" or "in memory" of someone. Meanwhile the "in memory" plaques adjacent to the Children's Wall were almost all sold out.

Board membership had become very large during the late 1990s, peaking at 40 or more in some years. Meetings were often unwieldy, and the high emotions displayed on issues, at times even on the most mundane decision, assumed an almost constant reality at meetings. As Board Secretary, Marion Reiss often struggled to take down every word in the notes for the minutes. On one occasion, Rhoda Freidman, looking over her shoulder, said to her: "I wondered how you were going to write this up." In those days, minutes were read aloud at the subsequent meeting for approval, and the minutes were often applauded for their common-sense recollection of what had happened the month before. Marion was insistent that in the typing process, no changes be made to the minutes above her signature. No one was allowed to add comments or report events that happened subsequent to the meeting. This had not been the policy beforehand, and at first Barbara Grau, as executive director, objected to not having veto power; in the end, the integrity of the minutes remained untouched.

During this period, the suggestion was made to hold bi-monthly instead of monthly meetings. Over the next few years, the Board experimented with bi-monthly and quarterly spaced meetings, with Executive meetings in-between.

One recurring issue involved coverage of the Center on Sundays for drop-in visitors and students doing research. Many Board members enjoyed manning the Center on Sundays, but it was a problem for others. Finally a policy was instituted that members could either donate a Sunday to the Center or contribute $50 so that someone could be hired to do so. This policy stayed in place for many years until the need was seen to pay someone every Sunday. About this time, too, another part-time employee was added to the Center: Ed Krupnik, who served as bookkeeper.

An unusual fund-raising activity was added to the Center's lineup of activities in 1998. With active prompting by Ruby Josephs, Chairman of the Board and a motorcycle enthusiast, a "Motorcycle Run" was held. Bike clubs across the region were invited to join in a bike ride for the "Center." It was quite a sight to see the various motorcycle clubs with their insignias revving their motors and zooming into the parking lot early on a Sunday morning. The members of the Board learned, however, how to sign them in and get them on their way (after coffee and bagels, of course.) The "Run" made money for the Center and received some nice publicity, as well.

The Center's further physical expansion was being planned, with Jeff and Stuart Weinberger, sons of one of the original donors, Sam Weinberger, taking on the task of supervising the building project. The new area would house a permanent "Liberators Exhibit." A private groundbreaking ceremony, arranged by Ruby Josephs, was held for this wing and honored two major donors, the Julie Stern and Weinberger families. Although this limited ceremony was done to save time according to Josephs, many members felt that the Board should have been invited, especially since the press had attended.

However, the formal opening of the Liberators Exhibit and the new wing was very well attended, with many dignitaries present. Memories, though, were already beginning to fade as was later brought to the attention of the Board by a letter from Assemblyman Sam Colman, who quoted the phrase, "the ultimate love is the love that can be taken for granted," to illustrate his complaint: none of the

acknowledgments made during the event mentioned his or Assemblyman Gromack's grants or any of Colman's prior support, all of which had been so crucial to the initial construction of the Center.

It was an old story for Harry Reiss, whose role in starting the Center was not only not mentioned but probably unknown to many of the new Board members. The leather-bound pictorial and newspaper-clipping history of the Center that Marion Reiss had put together in 1999 and presented to the Center as a gift from the Reisses lay in a closed cabinet in the Director's office; there

had been a vague promise that some day it would be taken downstairs and displayed. It never was. Many years later, when a new director and a new secretary were moving files around, the album was discovered. The Director Tanja Sarett and the President Paul Galan both called Marion to say that they had found a treasure of information about the Center. That the album still lies deep in

some cabinet provided, in some ways, the impetus for the present volume.

There were a number of successful fundraising events in 1998-99: a Journal-Dinner honoring Jacques Gerstenfeld, Karl Hess and Ilse Loeb, a Purim concert featuring the Hester Street players, a Cocktail party honoring Clarkstown Supervisor Holbrook, as well as the sale of bricks and plaques. The Hidden Children Exhibit had been loaned out to several places, including Albany College, and Vineland and Springfield, New Jersey. Each visit was accompanied by a talk by either Ilse Loeb or Max Goudsmith. What was unforeseen about this exhibit was possible mutilation; after one particular loan, it was returned with significant damage. Fundraising events were generally well attended; however, often the expenses cut heavily into revenue for the Center. For example, one event grossed $2500, but the outlay came to $2000. The price of the Journal-Dinner was raised from $36 to $54. Grants pledged in 1999 were as follows: $3000--Town of Ramapo; $1500--Clarkstown; $7500--Rockland County; $6000-Jewish Federation. New York State grants, pledged by Senator Thomas Morahan, amounted to $50,000 plus $10,000 for Teachers' Seminars; these were in addition to those initiated by Assemblyman Colman - $10,000; and Assemblyman Alex Gromack - $10,000.

At a meeting chaired by Felicia Hirshfeld in 1999, a unanimous decision was taken to revise the Center's By-Laws to include all past-presidents as members of the Executive Board. There was an attempt that year to institute a Board membership fee of $180. After meeting with strong objections by some members of the Board, the proposal was reworded to make this sum an umbrella figure for all donations in a "give or get (raise money)" kind of format. In other words, Board members would have to either donate or raise funds up to a certain amount to fulfill their financial obligation. The issue was put aside at the time although it was to come up again in the future, when it was incorporated with a much higher dollar obligation.

At the turn of the century, the Holocaust Center Board consisted of 43 active members and 14 members of the Board of Governors as follows: Rubin Josephs, Chairman of the Board; Max Goudsmith, President; Karl Hess, Belle Rosenbaum, Merri Rosenbaum, Gloria Zeisel, Vice-Presidents; Dr. Joel Feldman, Mark Weidman, Treasurers; Marion Reiss, Secretary. Past-Presidents - Lillian Adler, Anne Katz, Harry Reiss, Al Kirsch. Executive Director - Barbara Grau.

The Board of Trustees included Cynthia Becher, Carol Berkman, Estelle Eisenkraft, Rhoda Friedman, Norman Garfield, Leon Ginsburg, Felicia Hirshfeld, Mimi Kirsch, Susan Klein, Mark Miller, Alan Koss, Eleanor Kuhns, Rose Levy, Ilse Loeb, Sara Muschel, Eva Nordhauser, Judy Pesetsky, Tobe Rebhun, Faye Rosen, Esther Schulman, Judith Siegelbaum, Sid Silver, Sam Simon, Maxine Stern, Myer Tulkoff, Jeffrey Weinberg, Stanley Weiner, Estelle Weitzner, and Phyllis Wind.

The Board of Governors listed Warren Berbit, Hon. Sam Colman, Robert Finkelstein, Rabbi Louis Frishman, Jacques Gerstenfeld, Kenneth Gribetz, Georgine Hyde, Joel Sheinert, Rabbi Moses Tendler, Hon. Alan Thompson, Joseph Warburg, Sam Weinberger, Bernard Wiener, and Henry Zeisel.

Mark Weidman was soon added to the Board at the recommendation of Harry Reiss, who had met him when Weidman was a guest speaker at Reiss's Holocaust History class at Rockland Community College. Weidman had been a young teenager when arrested as a Pole and taken to one of the death camps. He hid his Jewish identity throughout, but there was one guard who suspected him of being a Jew and one day confronted him in front of everyone.

Mark told the story of how he grabbed the guard and punched him saying, "Don't you ever call me a 'dirty Jew' again. You are a Jew." The guard left him alone after that although he could as easily have killed him. Mark recalled that after the war, he and his wife were walking on a street in Paris when this same man crossed his path. "I knew you were a Jew," he spat at the young couple. Mark Weidman seldom spoke of his experiences, but Harry encouraged him to speak to school groups and to record his story.

The Journal-Dinner for the year 2000 held on June 25 at the New City Jewish Center, honored Lillian Adler and Judith Siegelbaum. The keynote speaker was a survivor, Ernest Michel; and a special presentation was made to New York State Senator Morahan.

The year 2000 ushered in a notable change: the Center applied for a name change to "Holocaust Museum and Study Center." It was hoped that changing to museum status under the New York State Division of Museums would help the Center to qualify for more grant monies from diverse sources.

A unique program was being planned for January 15, 2001 – Martin Luther King Day. For several months, a committee consisting of Harry and Marion Reiss and Barbara Grau for the Center and Stella Marrs and Dr. Susan Gordon for the Martin Luther King Multi-Purpose Center in Spring Valley, had planned a dual program on "Confronting Racism" for that day. With the aim of promoting understanding and tolerance, the program at the MLK Center featured the film, "From Swastika to Jim Crow," which was followed by addresses by its film maker, Lori Cheatle, and by Mrs. Carolyn Goodman, mother of Andrew Goodman, one of the three young men killed by the Ku Klux Klan in Mississippi in 1964 while trying to register African-American citizens to vote. Marion met Mrs. Goodman after the latter had spoken at the Museum of Jewish Heritage and arranged for her to participate at the MLK Day event.

Mrs. Goodman devoted much of her life to promoting understanding between Jews and African-Americans. At the age of 80 plus, she was as lively as could be; in fact, at the conclusion of her talk, she announced she was traveling to Washington, D. C., to petition on behalf of a congressional vote. The final speaker at the MLK event was Professor John Herz of Howard University. A kosher dinner was served at the Martin Luther King Center.

Harry Reiss had arranged for the East Ramapo School District to provide transportation, and the entire assemblage then moved across town to the Rockland Center for Holocaust Studies, where the program took on a different tone. The keynote speaker was the well-known civil rights activist and community leader Ken Mercer, who stressed the evils of the African-American experience. He was followed by Coni Williams, who spoke about her own experiences in taking advantage of opportunities in Rockland County and of working with youth defendants in the newly founded Rockland Youth Court. Because of the lateness of the hour, the second workshop and tour of the Center had to be curtailed. Nonetheless, the committee felt it had blazed pathways for future programs that would promote dialogue and understanding in the very diverse community of Rockland County through these two venerable Rockland institutions of tolerance. The program turned out to be costly; still, the committee made several attempts afterwards to reengage the Martin Luther King Center in dialogue regarding organizing another event. Unfortunately, this type of program has not been replicated to this day.

The Kristallnacht Commemoration that year moved from the Center to the grounds of the County Courthouse in New City and included a "Vigil for Tolerance," after which the crowd went to the Clarkstown Town Hall auditorium for a program of speakers. In future years, the format changed to an annual Kristallnacht candle-lighting vigil held on the steps of the County Courthouse.

MARTIN LUTHER KING
MULTI-PURPOSE CENTER, INC.

ROCKLAND CENTER FOR
HOLOCAUST STUDIES

Co-Sponsoring

CONFRONTING RACISM

MONDAY JANUARY 15, 2001
8:30 A.M. TO 5:00 P.M.

Morning Program

Martin Luther King Multi-Purpose Center, Inc.
110 Bethune Blvd. Spring Valley, New York 10977

Registration and Continental Breakfast
8:30-9:15 am

Welcome
Dr. Susan G. Gordon
Martin Luther King Multi-Purpose Center, Inc.

Introduction
Ms. Barbara Grau
Rockland Center for Holocaust Studies

FILM: FROM SWASTIKA TO JIM CROW

SPEAKERS:

Ms. Lori Cheatle
Film Maker
Dr. Carolyn Goodman
President Andrew Goodman Foundation
Prof. John Herz
Howard University

Lunch
Eli's Bagels
Noon- 12:40pm
Martin Luther King Multi-Purpose Center

Shuttle buses available for transportation to
Rockland Center for Holocaust Studies
Made possible by Jason Friedman,
East Ramapo Central School District

Afternoon Program

Rockland Center for Holocaust Studies, Inc.
17 S. Madison Avenue, Spring Valley, NY 10977

1-1:30pm

Keynote Speaker: Ken Mercer
Executive Director
Edenwald-Gun Hill Neighborhood Center

Workshop I 1:30-2:45 pm

Session A

Undoing Racism
Ms. Coni Williams and
Community Activist

Session B

Film- Hate.Com
Barbara Grau

Workshop II 3:00-4:15 pm

Session A

Tour: Holocaust Museum
Barbara Grau

Session B

African-Carribean-
American Experience
Ken Mercer and
Dr. Stella Marrs

Closing 4:15-5:00pm
Ms. Barbara Grau
Dr. Stella Marrs
Honorable Harry Reiss

176

Esther Ingber assumed the position of Center President in 2001, with Leon Ginsburg and Tobe Rebhun replacing Belle Rosenbaum and Merri Rosenbaum as Vice-Presidents. Rubin Josephs remained chairman of the Board. It was not until much later that the progression from Executive Vice-President to President to Chairman of the Board was uniformly set in place. It was during Ingber's term of office that the Center's name was officially changed to the Holocaust Museum and Study Center.

New stationery was printed and, for a time, the names of large donors were also included on the stationery. Fundraising continued to be a major concern, especially that year, since there was no Journal-Dinner. In future years, the dinner would be held every year, but in 2001 it was still conducted every other year; the feeling was that donors would not be as inspired to give every single year. Various fundraising activities were tried, one of which was a tea-bag mailing, with the tea bags being donated by Pathmark; another activity was a festive Hannukah concert, preceded by a special reception and followed by a dessert party.

During the course of the year, twelve trustees resigned either because they were moving out of the area or for personal reasons. By 2002, the number of trustees, not including officers, amounted to only 14. In spite of its new museum status, the Center at this point seemed to have reached a plateau from which it could not budge. More and more emphasis was being placed on fundraising, and less on the Center's mission itself. The growing sense of dissatisfaction among some members was expressed by Max Goudsmith, who in his farewell speech to the board, emphasized the importance of friendship and working together.

✡ Board of Trustees of
The Holocaust Museum & Study Center ✡

Journal-Dinner honoring Max Goudsmith and the survivors June 6 2002

178

CHAPTER 11

CHANGE AND CHALLENGES, 2002-2007

It was in fact, a time of changes for the Center: Barbara Grau, the executive director retired. The Holocaust Remembrance Day program which had culminated each year in the huge, emotionally charged, county-wide commemoration event, morphed into a series of experiential dramatic presentations in smaller, separate venues; by their very nature, however, they could not generate the county-wide enthusiasm that had characterized the previous commemorations. Cognizance of this fact was manifested by Max Goudsmith, who recalled the success and huge turnouts of county-wide commemorations and expressed the wish that Harry Reiss would reactivate them. In fact at the Remembrance Day Commemoration held on April 14, 2002, Harry was asked to make the introductory remarks for the program held at the RCC Cultural Arts Center. As though to prove the point, the Center's Executive Director at the time, Moses Weintraub, commented that Harry's remarks "have touched everyone" and invited him to deliver the opening remarks again at the 2003 program.

The Center was spending large sums of money on its various programs. The Board, to deal with its large membership, organized a committee system to undertake work in smaller groups, but this actually had the effect of dividing Board members instead of uniting them. Harry Reiss, who had been the emotional force in promoting the ideals of the Center, had lost his vehicle for expressing those principles when he lost the chairmanship of the annual Remembrance Day event. Money problems also caused tension. Ruby Josephs, one of the prime money-raisers for the Center, expressed disappointment that his efforts were not being matched. In fact, despite the efforts of individual and groups of Board members, donations remained scarce and grants were not increasing. In addition, unlike the early days, when only token honorariums were paid to speakers and goods and services were donated to the Center or sold at discounted prices, the full price now had to be paid for everything. At times, commitments were made for speakers or events that could not be met, and therefore efforts had to be made to find additional sponsors after the fact.

The Center's Board in 2002 consisted of the following officers: Esther Ingber – President; Len Ginsburg, Karl Hess, and Merri Rosenbaum – Vice-Presidents; Joel Feldman and Mark Koller – Treasurers; Marion Reiss–Secretary; and these Board members: Jerry Bergson, Carol Berkman, Rhoda Friedman, Leonard Greenberg, Eleanor Kuhns (who represented the Finkelstein Library), Rose Levy, Sara Muschel, Eva Nordhauser, Judy Pesetzky, Belle Rosenbaum, Esther Schulman Judith Siegelbaum, Jeff Weinberger, Stanley Wiener, Phyllis Wind, and Gloria Zeisel.

A new Journal-Dinner honoring past President Max Goudsmith was planned for June 6, 2002. Harry Reiss chaired the Journal committee and asked a new member of the Board, Len Greenberg, to co-chair the Journal with him. The guest speaker was Congressman Sam Gejdenson, and a special recognition was given to Scott Vanderhoef, the Rockland County Executive. After hearing the story of hidden children in Holland at the dinner, Mr. Vanderhoef got up and, to thunderous applause, said: "Today, I am proud to be a Dutchman."

When Barbara Grau first declared her intention to retire, the Center Board had selected Moses Weintraub, a soon-to-be retired New York City social studies teacher, to take over as Director when Grau retired in June. The plan was for him to intern during the months of May and June so as to be ready for the job by July 2002. Meanwhile, his wife died quite suddenly before he assumed the position. Soon after taking on the job officially in September, Weintraub suggested the need for an educational director to oversee the school groups and also assist with grant writing. The Board asked Grau to return and take on the position of educational director, since she had years of experience at the Center. There had not been time to clarify the division of responsibilities between the two positions and Weintraub resigned in May 2003. Barbara Grau now found herself back in her old position as director.

Money seemed to be rushing out faster than it was coming in. Proposing an exhibit of his experiences in Oswego, New York, the camp established for Jewish refugees by the U.S. government in 1944 on Lake Ontario, Walter Greenberg asked the Center for an initial outlay of $5,000 to help defray the $15,000 cost of matting the artworks. The ensuing exhibit proved very successful, but there was a misunderstanding about who owned it. The Center expected it to be part its permanent museum exhibition much like the Hidden Children Exhibit; however, this was not how Greenberg saw matters, and in fact the exhibit did not remain with the Center.

The 2003 Board reflected a desire to update and reenergize, with a clear line of succession in place and the induction of new members: Simon Bergson, Brenda Greenberg, Felicia Hirshfeld, Eli Josephs, Hon. Shirley Lasker, Sandy Parris, Tobe Rebhun, Jerry Stulberg, and Stuart Weinberger. A festive collation was held, and gifts were given out to reelected officers. Marion Reiss was pleased to receive a fine new pen, presumably for taking minutes, but it began to leak when she tried it out. Observing this, one new trustee remarked that it was not a good sign for the new members. However, Board Chairman Ruby Josephs, visibly pleased with the new trustees, remarked: "Now I know that the future of the Board is in good hands." Ten years later, of the new members inducted that evening, only Stuart Weinberger remained an active member.

Karl Hess became President in 2003, with Jeff Weinberger, Carl Berkman, and Leon Ginsburg as Vice-Presidents. Len Greenberg became Treasurer, a post he would hold together with Mark Koller until Greenberg's resignation in 2010. Marion Reiss remained Secretary, and Belle Rosenbaum and Gloria Zeisel were curators of the Center's museum. Carol Berkman had previously started a program called Café Europa for survivors to meet and discuss various issues. Sometimes with shaky attendance, it nevertheless persisted and became a mainstay of the Center, now called the Museum. Belle Rosenbaum donated her collection of "Monkey Says, Monkey Does" sculptures to the Museum, together with a sizable donation. The collection is still exhibited at the Museum. A fundraising project that brought in unexpected revenue was the publication of a cookbook by the Museum, entitled *Recipes and Remembrances*. It remains a big seller today. The Center's staff at this point included Barbra Grau, Executive Director; Barbara Posner Klipper, Grau's assistant; Roberta Lieman, Secretary; and Ed Krupnik, Bookkeeper.

The annual Remembrance Day program in April 2003, held at Rockland Community College, featured Dr. Susan Zuccotti, who spoke about her latest book, *Under His Very Windows: The Vatican and the Holocaust in Italy*. Though an excellent scholar and speaker, Zuccotti could not come on the date of Yom HaShoah (Holocaust Remembrance Day); in consequence, the program was held on another evening, somewhat diluting its effect and, perhaps for that reason, the turnout was disappointingly small. Despite the audience's participation, the evening bore little resemblance to the commemorations that had been a staple of the Center in past years.

That April, also, featured Annette Dumbach , author of "The White Rose-Shattering the German Night", who had led a workshop at the Center's 3rd Educator's conference, as the keynote speaker at the Rockland Community College Yom HaShoah Program chaired by Harry Reiss and David Beisel.

The Hidden Children Exhibit was loaned out to the Rodeph Shalom Temple in Manhattan; it was the first Holocaust program held there. The exhibit was also shipped to Naples, Florida.

Barbara Grau had made very clear her decision to retire finally in 2004, and a search committee was formed to find a new Director. Money-saving changes that were attempted included closing the Museum on Fridays and during the month of August. Sam Colman, now retired from the New York Assembly, had donated a sum of money to be used for an annual lecture series. Usually admission to these lectures was free, with a request for a voluntary donation. This year, however, a $5 admission was charged to defray the speaker's fee. The talk given by Thane Rosenbaum of Columbia University and author of *Second Hand Smoke* was well attended despite the fee and the abstruse nature of his presentation. The year ended sadly with the sudden passing of Mark Weidman and with Max Goudsmith's illness.

The beginning of 2004 was marked by the active search for a new director. By March, the Search Committee had narrowed its choices and was ready to recommend Rabbi Michael Gisser, recently the coordinator of Jewish student activities at Farleigh Dickinson University. The position was ultimately offered to Rabbi Gisser, who would combine all organizational and fundraising efforts with the Center's Educational Program. Rabbi Gisser became the first full-time Director of the Center, with all the financial responsibility that such a position entailed. Rockland's Holocaust Museum and Study Center was now a fully functioning institution with issues of payroll, building, and maintenance to consider in addition to its educational and commemorative programs.

With Barbara Grau's imminent retirement, it was decided that the Journal-Dinner planned for June would honor both her and the Center's past president, Esther Ingber. The glatt kosher dinner was held at the Rockleigh Country Club, and U.S. Congresswoman from New York Nita Lowey received a "Woman of Distinction Award." Lillian Adler chaired the Journal committee. It was the first Dinner at which Harry Reiss was not either the Center's Director, Honoree, President, or Journal Chairman. A photo of Harry and Marion at the event reflects their relaxation at this serendipitous situation. Barbara Grau was duly

Harry and Marion Reiss

congratulated on her retirement with the additional thanks for the many years that she had worked a full-time job for the Center while receiving a part-time salary. One thing was made clear: her tenure had been —in understatement—a bargain for the Museum.

The new director lost no time in trying to make the Center a more modern and interactive facility. One of his projects was to institute the use of credit cards to pay dues and donations. He also made an immediate impact on the press, publicizing events and activities. A boat ride on the "Commander" up the Hudson River, organized by Fundraising Vice-President Jeff Weinberger, solidified the positive energy felt by the Board. Other events in the course of the next few months included a War Veterans Program, a Colman lecture featuring Rochelle Seidel speaking about the Ravensbruck concentration camp, a food and wine exposition fundraiser, and a showing of film "Paperclips."

A few months before Gisser's assuming the directorship, a teenager convicted of a hate crime had been mandated to do community service at the Center; he visited the Museum, attended a Café Europa meeting, spoke with survivors, and later submitted an essay about his experiences. So impressive was this experience for him that his parents wrote a letter of thanks to the Center. Gisser worked to make the Holocaust Museum and Study Center the official voice against incidents of anti-Semitism in Rockland County. He persisted in this idea and eventually convinced the County's Board of Rabbis to designate the Center as the reporting agency for all incidents of bias in Rockland County and the address for setting protocols for fighting anti-Semitism in the county.

In December 2004, then-U.S. Senator Hillary Clinton, accompanied by New York Assemblywoman Ellen Jaffe, visited the Center and spoke about the need to eradicate anti-Semitism and bias. Board members were invited, and the Reisses, who had met the Senator in the past, were pleased to have a few minutes to speak with her. It was strictly a Center event, so members of the Board were mildly surprised when some of the elected officials in the area complained about not having been invited. Everyone realized afterwards that the

Harry Reiss, Lillian Adler, Senator Clinton

185

Michael Gisser, Harry Reiss, Ellen Jaffe, Hillary Clinton

fact that Harry Reiss, a town councilman, and his wife had been photographed at the event gave the impression that only a few Ramapo officials had been invited. Harry Reiss was there in his capacity as a founder and trustee of the Center, not as a town official.

The new Board of Directors was inducted at the December 2004 Board meeting. Jeff Weinberger was elected President, with Mark Koller, Felicia Hirshfeld, Sandi Parris, and Tobe Rebhun, Vice-Presidents. Leonard Greenberg continued as Treasurer, and Marion Reiss as Secretary. Trustees were Jerry and Simon Bergson, Carol Berkman, Steve Gold, Brenda Greenberg, Eli Josephs, Belle Rosenbaum, Merri Rosenbaum, Nat Wasserstein, Stuart Weinberger, Phyllis Wind, David Zedeck, Gloria Zeisel, and Erica Grodin (representing the Library in place of Eleanor Kuhns). Cliff Wood, President of Rockland Community College, would join the Board during the year. Rubin Josephs this year, too, expressed his satisfaction in seeing the torch passed to a new generation; he and Sam Weinberger had been survivors and were early donors to the Center.

A question was raised about this time in regard to a possible legal limitation on the number of Board members for a New York non-profit organization. It was thought to be around 25, a number often exceeded by the Center. The question would arise again in later years, when the Board's membership became smaller.

By the beginning of 2005, a new energy was definitely felt on the Board and at the Center in general. Yet there were also murmurings of discontent with the status quo. Talk began of moving the whole facility to another location, possibly the new JCC Campus in West Nyack. Harry scribbled down a series of questions about this on a scrap of yellow paper:

Who would benefit? What would be the cost? What would they want from us? How would we have to change? How would it affect the goals of the Center?

He had always felt that its present location, as part of the Finkelstein Library, the largest in the Hudson Valley Region, was the most central location for the Center. Discussions of moving either to the JCC campus or to the Rockland Community College site continued till 2012, when it was decided to move the Museum in part or in whole to the campus of Rockland Community College.

Meanwhile, the Finkelstein Library itself had suffered a defeat of its budget; at the same time, it was seeking to expand its space. Some tension was developing between the Library and the Center, but a rapprochement meeting led by Harry Reiss and Michael Gisser for the Center and Bob Devino for the Library resulted in a new declaration of partnership and good will between the two entities. Karl Hess subsequently volunteered his services as architect to help design the alleyway between the two buildings, and the Library graciously agreed to have its snowplowing service continue to clear the sidewalk in front of the Center.

One of Michael Gisser's main projects that first year of his directorship was to plan the Center's participation in the 60th anniversary of the Liberation March of the Living to Poland, with an optional trip to Israel to follow, to be held from May 3-May 13, 2005. Scheduled as an adult group activity and as part of a nationwide program, the March proved a turning point not only for the personal experiences of those Board members who participated but also for the Center itself, as it brought in new members with fresh enthusiasm for its message and mission.

The Center had in past years subsidized individual students who applied to join the march. This year, several subsidies were available, but most participants paid their own way. The group was led by Michael Gisser; members of the Board who went were Marion Reiss, Rose Levy, and Carol Berkman, who was invited in her role as social worker. Three others who attended and were to become very involved with the leadership of the Center: Paul Adler, who attended with his two teen-age daughters; Alan Moskin, who had been among the liberators of the camps; and Paul Galan, who came along as a videographer. Paul's transformation from documenter of the trip to full participant came to light at one break-out session during the trip when he declared to the group that he had been a child survivor himself. So devoted was Paul Galan to the Museum that he was ultimately elected President. When the Rockland contingent visited the site of the infamous ghetto in Lodz, Poland, it made a quick detour for Rose Levy to visit the apartment building in which she had lived after the war. While the rest of the group remained on the bus to allow Rose her private emotions in visiting her past, they did go along with her to visit the Jewish cemetery at Lodz. Levy looked for her family graves as the rest of the group was shown the mass unmarked gravesites of those who had died in the ghetto or been murdered after the war when they attempted to rebuild their lives in Poland.

The "March" visited Auschwitz-Birkenau, Majdanek, Chelmo, and the sites of the Warsaw and Lodz Ghettos. One of the participants was an 83-year-old survivor of Auschwitz, Sylvia Kagan. She described Auschwitz as: "Hell – 12 women sleeping on one level of a bunk, no food, no water at times." She recalled the smells of burning flesh and the flames from the crematorium. Toward the end of the war, she was transported in a cattle car, and her hand was injured during a bombing. It was later amputated. When the group walked through Auschwitz, Kagan was able to point out different barracks and landmarks that she remembered. Her first words upon entering Birkenau were: "I don't remember any grass here." One of the stories she told the group reverberated even more because of the matter-of-factness of her description. There were two electrified fences around Auschwitz, she recalled. The Polish population would walk right up to the fence. Occasionally, some people would toss food into the camp, but often a roll or an apple fell between the two fences. Once she saw a girl ever so carefully reach between the fences to retrieve a roll; "within seconds, smoke was pouring out of every orifice of her body.... I never went near those fences although we were starving all of the time."

Kagan had hoped to find Lager C, where she had been incarcerated 60 years before, and someone did try to find it with her; however, the group's time there was coming to a close and they had to leave to catch a train before she could find it. Although most of the group's travel was by bus, Michael Gisser conceived the plan that since Jews had been brought to Auschwitz by train to be murdered, it would be a powerful symbol for the Rockland group to *leave by* train as free people. Most of the group was not so enamored by the idea, since it meant a long walk to the station (the trains no longer coming up to the camp gate).

As it happened, a strange phenomenon occurred on the train, an event so incongruous that it bears mentioning. The group was divided into compartments seating eight. The horrors of what had just been seen created an oppressive atmosphere as the passengers took their seats. Suddenly one person began to laugh and told a funny story unrelated to anything that was happening. Almost on cue, the others

189

Survivor Sylvia Kagen points to location where she lost her hand when the cattle car she was in was bombed over 60 years ago.

Haifa lecturer Israel Ne'eman with March of the Living participants-(L-R) Zahava Friedman, Elaine Silverberg, Marvin Baum, Naomi Stauber, Beth Nivin, Rose Levy, Rabbi Michael Gisser, Susan Krochmal, Lee Krochmal, Marion Reiss, Alan Moskin, Yisrael Ne'eman and Dr. Lawrence Lehman picked up on the story and continued with what might have appeared most inappropriate jesting. The jollity continued for some time, and was almost infectious. When the train stopped and the passengers of the compartment disembarked, everyone again became silent, withdrawn into their own thoughts. The same somber mood that had enveloped them when they had boarded the train, returned. So far as Marion Reiss, one of those in that compartment, could recall, no one ever spoke of this again. A year later, at a Colman lecture, held on March 23, 2006, the lecturer, historian Kenneth Libo referred to "Humor and the Holocaust." Many in the audience thought the title irreverent; remembering this incident, however, Marion wondered whether it did not indeed reflect some deep psychological response of the mind when confronting the evidence of incomprehensible evil.

So great was the bonding on that emotional trip that at the Center's next Journal-Dinner, in June 2005, honoring Tobe Rebhun in memory of her parents, and the Liberators, the entire group from the Center that had participated in the March of the Living was seated together with their spouses at a special table.

The Remembrance Day program, held mid-week that year, was chaired by Mark Koller. Harry Reiss was co-chairing the program for Rockland Community College, and it was suggested that he combine the two ceremonies in following years.

Marion Reiss suggested a creating a Museum Gift Shop and, together with Esther Ingber, Roberta Lieman, and Anne Katz, scouted out possible products for sale. Jeff Weinberger donated some display cases. The shop functioned for a while, with most of the sales being made to student groups and consisting of low-budget items. More expensive items were sold to Board members after meetings. The bookkeeping for the shop, however, was left in the air, since there was no staff to take care of it; ultimately, all revenues were merged. After about a year, the gift shop changed to a book shop, using the same display cases, but it too declined for lack of staff. Barbara Posner had resigned soon after Barbara Grau left, and Roberta Lieman was now the Center's full-time secretary.

A new interactive exhibit, "The Hiding," was prepared by David Lenik and partly funded by a grant received from State Senator Morahan. Using earphones and blindfolds, students would experience the simulated feelings of children hiding from the Nazis. It became one of the most powerful tools for teaching about the Holocaust to school children.

The Kristallnacht commemoration ceremony was held that year at the County courthouse in New City on November 9, 2005. The date fell on a Wednesday, one night after the election for Ramapo Supervisor and Town Council. Although Harry Reiss was successful in being reelected, it had been a difficult campaign and he was exhausted. There was a Town board meeting scheduled for that night, but it was agreed that Harry should first represent the town at the ceremony and afterwards return to the meeting. The rainy weather and sweeping winds made any kind of outside ceremony impossible, and the courthouse was opened so that the ceremony could take place inside for the first and only time. Despite his fatigue, Reiss spoke as he had done every year since the first commemoration in 1988:

"As a founder and past president of the Holocaust Museum and Study Center, and as a Councilman of the Town of Ramapo, I am honored to participate in this Vigil of Remembrance on the 67th anniversary of Kristallnacht, the Night of Broken Glass. Kristallnacht shattered freedom and showed the world that a government would no longer protect its people, protect civil rights, or guarantee law and order.

"On November 10, 1988, we held our first commemoration of the Night of Broken Glass at the Holocaust Museum. One of our speakers at that event remembered, as a young boy living next to a synagogue in Munich, [how] storm troopers knocked down the door of his apartment, threw furniture out the window, and took his father away. Later, the synagogue next door went up in flames. Unfortunately, bigotry and hate are still with us. It is up to us to react strongly with education and commitment. We must use the lessons of history to make sure that the horrors of the past are never repeated in any place for any group of people. Kristallnacht reminds us that 'indifference and inertia are the handmaidens of bigotry.' Eternal vigilance is the price of liberty."

The next night, Harry attended the Holocaust Center's Board meeting and presented the slate of new officers.

The year 2005 ended on a very high note at the annual Board meeting with the showing of a stirring video, created by Paul Galan, showing some of the highlights of the March of the Living trip. The synergy of the group was apparent and contagious to all who saw the film. The Board's officers remained largely in place for 2006: Rubin Josephs, Honorary Chairman; Karl Hess, Chairman of the Board; Jeff Weinberger, President; Tobe Rebhun and Felicia Hirshfeld, Vice-Presidents; Len Greenberg, Treasurer; Marion Reiss, Secretary. The new and returning members of the Board were Paul Adler, Paul Galan, Marvin Baum, Ernie Fromen, Rose Levy, Judy Pesetzky, and Sylvia Berkowitz. Alan Moskin would join the Board shortly thereafter.

Plans were also made to finally digitalize the popular Hidden Children exhibit so that it could be replicated on lightweight roll-up screens that were easier to transport.

Continuing the momentum of the previous months, the Board considered possible honorees for its next Journal-Dinner. Following a suggestion that a broad base of in-house honorees might bring in the most dinner attendees and the most journal ads, it was decided to honor the "Founders" of the Center. The only problem was that no one seemed to agree on who the founders were: Did founders mean the original three: Harry Reiss, Harold Siegelbaum, and Georgine Hyde? Or did they also include Sam Colman, who brought the subject to the County Legislature? What about the builders: Rubin Josephs, Joe Adler, Sam Weinberger? Every time a list was promulgated, a new name was suggested, some of whom had not actually joined the Board until much later. Perhaps Al and Mimi Kirsch should be included? Or Max Goudsmith, who did not come on board until 1994? Other category titles were then suggested to get around this problem: "Founders and Builders" or "Founders, Builders, and Donors."

The issue was still unresolved at the meeting of March 16, 2006, the last one Harry Reiss attended before suffering the severe stroke that would eventually prove fatal. More honoree names were added to the "Founders and Builders" list, among them the Zeisels and the Kirsches. It was not until much later that a decision was finally made to limit the list to all "founders and builders" in the first 18 years of the Center.

The dinner, with its many honorees, was held the night of September 12, 2006. With Harry Reiss hospitalized, Marion walked to the stage to pick up Harry's plaque. Beautifully embossed on gold leaf mounted on wood, it read:

HOLOCAUST MUSEUM AND STUDY CENTER

Is proud to honor

HARRY REISS

For his outstanding commitment to

Holocaust education and remembrance.

Unusual for such presentations, a phrase from the Ethics of the Fathers (*Pirke Avot*) was added:

"Who is wise? He who learns from all people

Who is mighty? The one who subdues the evil inclination (hate)

Who is rich? The one who rejoices in his portion

Who is honored? The one who honors other human beings"

The quotation was eerily appropriate to describe Harry's role in the Rockland Holocaust Center since its founding in 1979. He was full of knowledge on many subjects and shared his knowledge with his students and then with the entire community in the creation of the Center, an institution meant "to study the evils that happened so that they would never be repeated again." He learned from all people, sought their advice and assistance from the beginning, and always appreciated their participation.

Who is mighty? Subduing hate was Harry's mission. He wanted through the lessons of the Holocaust to alert future generations to the dangers of hatred of "any people of any religion, race or ethnic group." Even when faced with enmity against himself, Harry was ever the gentle man, seeking friendship and reconciliation even when it was not forthcoming in return.

Who is rich? Harry's mission was his wealth. He refused to take money for any of his work associated with his Holocaust activities. He was frugal with other people's money. The dissemination of ideas did not require wealth in his way of thinking, and the 18 years of his vibrant Remembrance Day programs bore testimony to this principle.

Who is honored? Harry was the first to give credit to others in any enterprise in which he was involved. Personal honor meant little to him; and if questioned about why his name was omitted from a particular program in which he had been involved, he would reply: "It does not matter – the work got done." His indifference to his own honor kept him an active and contributing member of the Center throughout the years, no matter his title or position.

Harry's work did "get done." The Rockland Center for Holocaust Studies renamed The Holocaust Museum and Study Center of Rockland County remains one of the few such institutions not located in a large city that continues its mission to this day.

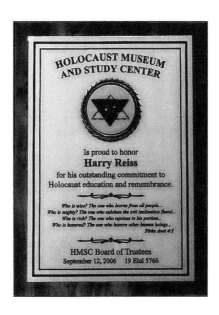

Epilogue

Harry Reiss's death was followed by that of Rubin Josephs within the year. Max Goudsmith had died previously. Al Kirsch also died. Rhoda Friedman passed on soon afterward. Ilse Loeb, Mark Koller, Esther Clifford, Leon Ginsburg, Norman Garfield, Barbara Grau, and Roberta Lieman all moved to different states.

Marion Reiss resigned her position as Secretary of the Board at the end of 2006 because she was completely involved with Harry's care at home. After his passing, she was invited to assume the position again and she acceded, serving until 2010. She continues as a trustee. Paul Galan became president and Alan Moskin vice-president. In the fall of 2007, Michael Gisser unexpectedly resigned and moved to another state.

Lisa Stenchover, a former Center volunteer, was appointed Educational Director.

Ed Krupick resigned after moving out of the County and was replaced by Geri Myers.

Rabbi Rick Harkavy came from California to replace Michael Gisser and also to take over the teaching of Harry Reiss's course at Rockland Community College.

A Shloshim (a memorial observance on the 30th day after one's death) for Harry was held at the Center. The speakers who delivered eulogies included Rabbi Moses Tendler, Georgine Hyde, who had to be assisted to rise to the podium, County Executive Scott Vanderhoeff, Chairman of the New York State Legislature Harriet Cornell, Ramapo Councilman Ed Friedman, County Legislator Phil Soskin, past Center President Karl Hess, past Finkelstein Library Director, Sam Simon, Larry Kalish, Howard Spear, and Harry's daughter- in- law Mindy. Anne Katz, who had previously eulogized Harry, conceded her place on this occasion owing to the lateness of the hour. Harry's son, Rabbi Yona Reiss, conducted the program and presented a siyum (summary of a tractate of Talmud study). The family members had all spoken previously at the funeral.

Someone remembered that a festive meal during the week following the wedding of Harry Reiss's son, Yona to Mindy (a ceremonial period for a new couple known as Sheva Brachot) had been held in that very room. A plaque memorializing that happy occasion in 1999 was mounted adjacent to the Children's Wall.

Rabbi Harkavy resigned after a year and returned to California. He was temporarily replaced by Rabbi Michael Bierman, who had been director of the UJA some years before. After a search for a new director, the Board invited Tanja Sarett, who had been born in Germany and had worked at the Dachau Museum, to become Director. Tanja Sarett served as director until 2012.

In September 2012, after months of discussion and negotiations, a Memorandum of Understanding was signed by Dr. Cliff Wood for Rockland Community College and Paul Galan for the Holocaust Museum and Study Center to establish a presence of the Museum/Center at the college. This included office space, signage, use of meeting rooms and exhibit areas. Further relocation of the Center would depend on space availability at the college and the financial means to utilize that space for Museum exhibits.

The Journal-Dinners from 2007 through 2012 had the following honorees:

2007 – Brenda and Len Greenberg, Roberta Lieman

2008 – Dr. Sonya and Milton Shapiro, Drs. Susan and Edmund Gordon, Hon. Harriet Cornell.

2009 – Jeff and Judy Weinberger, Rabbi Morris Zimbalist, Rebecca Wetzel.

2010 – Ilse and John Lang, Cary Falber.

2011 – Ramapo Town Supervisor Christopher St. Lawrence, Alan Moskin.

2012 (Brunch) – Helene and Steve Gold, Rabbi Shmuel and Devorah Gancz, Lisa Suss, Brian Bassuk.

The Board of Trustees in 2012 consisted of the following officers: Chairman of the Board – Jeff Weinberger; President – Paul Galan; Vice-Presidents –Mona Litwak, Alan Moskin, Kristen Stavisky; Treasurer– Richard Weisman; and Secretary– Lisa Kozin.

Trustees were Paul Adler, Carol Berkman, David Fried, David Haas, Mikki Leader, Marion Reiss, Judah Shapiro, David Stern, David Tannenbaum, Stuart Weinberger, and Phyllis Wind. Ex officio past presidents included Lillian Adler, Anne Katz, and Esther Ingber. Library representative – Erica Grodin; Executive Director – Tanja Sarett.

Honorary Board (formerly the Board of Governors): Jerry Bergson, Simon Bergson, Steve Gold, Eli Josephs, Shirley Lasker, Belle Rosenbaum, Sharon Sasson, Cliff Wood, and Gloria Zeisel.

At the December 2012 meeting, a new slate of officers was elected: Chairman of the Board – Paul Galan; President – Kristen Stavisky; Treasurer – Richard Weisman; Vice-Presidents – Lisa Kozin, Mona Litwak, Alan Moskin; Recording Secretary – David Tanenbaum.

Trustees: Paul Adler, Carol Beckman, Amy Edelstein, David Fried, David Haas, Micki Leader, Marion Reiss, Judah Shapiro, David Stern, Stuart Weinberger, Phyllis Wind. Past presidents – Lillian Adler, Esther Ingber, Anne Katz, Jeff Weinberger. Honorary Board – Jerry Bergson, Simon Bergson, Steve Gold, Eli Josephs Dr. Cliff Wood, Shirley Lasker, Belle Rosenbaum, Sharon Sasson, Gloria Zeisel.

Finkelstein Library Representative – Evelyn Daks (to be replaced later by Library Board President, Richard Rothbard); Rockland Community College Representative – Dr. Cliff Wood,; Director of Development and Operations – Andrea Winograd.

As this volume goes to press, plans for consolidation of the Letter of Intent between RCC and the Holocaust Museum are under way with the goal to relocate all Museum exhibits to the College within two years. If this takes place as currently planned, the Rockland Center for Holocaust Studies will have come full circle from its beginnings as a conceptual course on the Holocaust proposed by Harry Reiss at RCC, and will begin a new phase of its history as a Holocaust Museum and Study Center at Rockland Community College.

Harry's Story

The Rockland Center for Holocaust Studies, now called the Holocaust Museum and Study Center, was the first such institution to be established in the Lower Hudson Region, including New York City. It started as one man's idea, conceived in the late 1970's, and it came to fruition as the creation of a handful of men and women in the 1980's. The Center continues as a viable, independent institution to this day.

Woven throughout is the story of one man, Harry Reiss, who was the proverbial "first" from which the entire cadre of supporters, co-leaders, and builders was to grow. Harry was a simple man, brought up in the Northeast Bronx, attending public schools and after-school Talmud Torah; he graduated from Evander Childs High School and then the City College of New York. His father had immigrated alone to the United States at the age of 11 to join two older brothers and became a presser in the family clothing business. Harry was always proud of the fact that his father had invented the first one-zipper snowsuit for children and held a patent on it until it became a universal item.

His mother was born in the United States but spent some of her childhood in Warsaw when her mother took the children back there. His maternal uncle was a graduate of the Columbia University Dental School at a time when quotas for Jews were still in place. Harry's teenage years were spent with many friends in the Bronx, participating in various Jewish youth organizations, including Young Judea. He remembered planting a "Victory Garden" during World War II, and perhaps this explains his lifelong interest in gardening. His friends called him "Herschel" long before Jewish names were popular in Jewish circles. Harry was slated to become a lawyer, and his one sibling and elder brother, Ed, a dentist. When the brother contracted fungal disease during his World War II army service, he was forced to switch to law. It was inconceivable in those days that two sons could enter the same profession; therefore, when Harry completed his army service at the time of the Korean War, he took advantage of the army educational plan, the G.I. Bill of Rights, and went back to City College to earn his Master's degree in Education. He continued with a Doctoral program at Columbia University Teachers College; however, although he fulfilled all course requirements, including the final test with the highest score of his group, he never completed his dissertation. Still, many of his students and those who knew his intellectual prowess often conferred the title of "Dr." upon him.

He first met his wife, Marion, at a break during a teaching examination for the New York City Board of Education. He was totally immersed in reviewing the material that he hardly noticed her. However, Marion was impressed enough to cajole a neighbor— Harry's family had moved to the West Bronx by that time—to reintroduce them.

Harry began his teaching career as a history teacher at George Washington High School in Manhattan, and quickly became the advisor for the "Little United Nations Wishing Well" and other school clubs. He was also very involved in the "Higher Horizons" project, in which students at risk were given enrichment classes and activities to the point that some gained acceptance to Ivy League colleges.

In those days, advancement in the New York City School system was by examination, and Harry moved upwards, scoring at the top of every list, first as a Guidance Counselor at Evander Childs High School, and then as Assistant Principal and Administrative Principal in District 11 in the Bronx. He ran the very first Drug Prevention program for high school students in New York State. While teaching history at George Washington High School, he also taught that subject in the afternoon session at the nearby Yeshiva University High School for Boys. His students remember him as a gentleman, an intellectual, and a caring teacher.

Meanwhile he and Marion had married and moved to Rockland County, where they raised three children. When Rockland Community College opened its doors, Harry became one of the first adjunct professors to be appointed to the staff, and continued to teach there for over forty years. He first suggested teaching a course on the Holocaust in the early 1970s, but the college administration initially rejected his proposal. Harry was not to be deterred, though, for he had begun to feel the need to do something to make sure that the story of the Holocaust was taught and remembered. By the end of the decade, he was authorized to develop the course on the History of the Holocaust, which he taught until his stroke in 2006. He was not a survivor; nor was he the child of survivors. As a matter of fact, his mother had been born in Boston. Nor was his wife a child of survivors. What, then, prompted this modest, heretofore private individual to become the dynamic force in creating a Holocaust Study Center and a program for commemoration of the Holocaust in Rockland County and beyond?

First, Harry was innately a scholar. He was a prodigious reader throughout his life. His knowledge was expansive, not only of history but of subjects as diverse as baseball and silent-screen movies. Years later, when as a Ramapo town councilman, he used to appear on Ramapo Supervisor Christopher St. Lawrence's' weekly TV show, "Ramapo Live," and could talk on almost any subject. He had also begun to attend little-known seminars and meetings among some of the earliest scholars of the Holocaust, such as Alexander Donat.

Most important for him was the true horror at what he always termed the "evil" of the Holocaust. His sensitivity to human pain was passionately aroused by examples of "man's inhumanity to man." In his personal life, his sensitivity to others and his compassion were integral to his personality. One of his trademarks as town councilman, an office to which he was elected five times after his retirement from the New York City School System, was his empathy and concern for all groups of people in Ramapo. His telephone number remained listed in the phone book throughout his tenure, and he never failed to answer a call, no matter how inconvenient or how difficult the situation.

He was also a religious man, who prayed three times a day.

It was natural, then, for Harry to react with passion and indignation at indifference to human suffering. In his address at every Remembrance Day program and on every other occasion related to the Holocaust, he would refer explicitly to the "unspeakable acts that took place on beautiful spring days in 1943, 1944, and 1945." He cited the story by Tad Borodski about the young man who turned his back for a moment to a disembarking trainload of Jews to find that, "in the time it took to throw a soccer ball, 3000 people had been put to death." Harry then added: "I have constantly kept in my mind's eye the picture of these millions of defenseless and innocent men, women, and children who were slaughtered in gigantic death factories set up specially to process human beings."

Harry then perhaps best summed up the reasons for his personal commitment to the study of the Holocaust: "This affront to all humanity must never be permitted to happen again. In my own way, in America, I feel we can utilize the study of these terrible events to prevent any recurrence here or anywhere. I believe very much that what John Curran [an Irish politician and orator to whom a statue is dedicated in Washington, D.C.] said in 1790 is still true 200 years later, that 'the condition upon which God has given liberty to man is eternal vigilance.'"

Afterword

The creation of the Rockland Center for Holocaust Studies in Spring Valley, New York, in 1979-80 presaged the establishment of such institutions by almost a score of years. The United States Holocaust Museum in Washington, D.C., for example, was opened in 1993, and the Museum of Jewish Heritage – A Living Memorial to the Holocaust in New York City in 1997.

From 1979 through the present time, the Rockland Center has served as the major Holocaust institution for commemoration, education, and leadership in the entire Hudson Valley region. For the first 18 years of the Center's existence, its annual Holocaust Remembrance Day programs drew an audience of 700 to 800 people and became a major vehicle for Holocaust historians, survivors, and community spokespeople to commemorate the horrors of those tragic years. Annual Holocaust commemorations have continued to bring the message of remembrance to the entire community.

The fact that the Center provided a local source of information, commemoration, and memorialization of that terrible and unique time in history was sufficient raison d'être for the writing of this book. The passion of the founders, most of whom are no longer here, was able to sustain its viability for more than thirty years and continues to inspire their successors.

The foremost task of the Rockland Holocaust Center was to educate the new generations, Jewish and non-Jewish, about the disintegration of humanity and the destruction of liberty that led to the annihilation of two thirds of European Jewry—men, woman, and children, some six million people. Thousands of schoolchildren from Rockland County and beyond have visited the Center over the decades of its existence, listened to testimonies of survivors, and participated in classroom discussions about man's inhumanity to man.

When the Nazi Party began the systematic denial of civil and human rights to Germany's Jewish population, very few public officials spoke up. It was this silence that enabled Hitler and the Nazi government to carry out their final solution. Harry Reiss understood that for people to plan the mass killing of other human beings, they first had to dehumanize their victims. In this connection, he would relate a story told by Susan Ferraro about a religious Jewish man in a dog cart:

A child asks: "Why is the man in a cart?"

The author replies: "Because they are taking him to a concentration camp. They are Nazis and he is Jewish."

"But why is he in a cart?"

"Because they want to humiliate him."

"But why do they want to humiliate him if they are going to kill him anyway?"

"Because if they treat him like an animal, they can do what they are doing. If they remember he is human, they won't be able to do it."

The work of the Rockland Center for Holocaust Studies, or Holocaust Museum and Study Center as it is now called, will continue whether it remains in its present location or, as is currently planned, moves to the campus of Rockland Community College. The access to a large venue with many classrooms, display areas, and conference rooms makes the move attractive to those who would like to see an expansion of the Center's activities. In addition, the presence of the Holocaust Center/Museum on a college campus will make it readily available not only to ten thousand visitors a year but to thirty thousand. Indeed, the few events the Center has sponsored on the RCC campus in recent years found many students in attendance, fulfilling assignments by their professors or just dropping in for the program. In observing the reactions of this new group of students to the Holocaust programs presented, we may glean new insights into how best to continue to bring the lessons of the Holocaust to a new generation. So there is much excitement and anticipation of continuing the work of the Holocaust Center at this new venue.

It was at RCC that Harry Reiss developed a course on the History of the Holocaust, one of the first of its kind in the academic world and one that perhaps sparked the idea of creating a Holocaust study center in Rockland County. Harry continued to teach the course at RCC until his stroke in 2006. In addition, the high-school curriculum he developed in conjunction with the college was adapted and utilized throughout the county's school districts.

Finally, it is hoped that this volume has effectively documented some of the efforts of the people who lived in the United States several decades after World War II to commemorate and remember the victims of the Holocaust, and to teach its lessons to new generations. It is in itself a phenomenon worth documenting, to observe the confluence of teachers, historians, survivors, and the children of survivors who came together in this effort. It was a moment of time that has passed into history, as the study of the

Holocaust has in recent years become more institutionalized, and the original historians and survivors are slowly passing from the scene.

As such, this story is a historical vignette of a particular time and place in Holocaust study and commemoration that will take its place in the historiography of the Holocaust. It is a story that should resonate in the history of Holocaust studies in the United States.